The Fragile Community:
Living Together With AIDS

Everyday Communication: Case Studies of Behavior in Context
Wendy Leeds-Hurwitz & Stuart J. Sigman, Series Editors

The Fragile Community: Living Together With AIDS

Mara B. Adelman
Seattle University

Lawrence R. Frey
Loyola University Chicago

LEA LAWRENCE ERLBAUM ASSOCIATES, PUBLISHERS
1997   Mahwah, New Jersey

Lawrence Erlbaum Associates, Inc., Publishers
10 Industrial Avenue
Mahwah, New Jersey 07430

Cover design by Mairav Salomon-Dekel

Library of Congress Cataloging-in-Publication Data

Adelman, Mara B.
    The fragile community: Living together with AIDS
/ Mara B. Adelman & Lawrence R. Frey.
        p. cm.
    Includes bibliographical references and index.
        ISBN 0-8058-1843-X (cloth : alk. paper). — ISBN
0-8058-1844-8 (pbk. : alk. paper)
        1. AIDS (Disease)—Patients—Social networks—Il-
linois—Chicago. 2. Self-help groups—Illinois—Chicago. 3. Group homes—Illinois—Chicago. I. Frey
Lawrence R. II. Title.
RC607.A26A3424 1996
362.1'969792'00977311—dc20   96-28452
                                                CIP

Books published by Lawrence Erlbaum Associates are
printed on acid-free paper, and their bindings are chosen
for strength and durability.

Printed in the United States of America
10 9 8 7 6 5 4 3 2 1

This book is dedicated to the spirit, vision, and devotion of
The Alexian Brothers of America

Standing in front of a statue of St. Alexius, Brother Joel (left) and Brother Boniface
(right) of the Alexian Order were on-site staff members for many years at Bonaventure
House until their deaths from cancer. Brother Don of the Franciscan Order (center) was
also on the staff for several years, and now works at a parish in Greenwood, Mississippi.
Their dedication and departures are felt deeply by all who knew them.

Contents

Editors' Preface

How does "community" develop? Once developed, how is it maintained? *The Fragile Community: Living Together With AIDS*, the fifth volume in the Everyday Communication series, provides some answers to these questions by looking at the example of a group of individuals initially similar only in their illness (AIDS), and in their place of residence (Bonaventure House in Chicago). The book describes those communication practices that enable these individuals to create and sustain community.

Mara Adelman and Lawrence Frey base their study on several years of combined qualitative and quantitative research. They introduce readers to a group of people facing the consequences of extreme physical illness (including social stigma and death) who turn to each other for social support. The authors look at how it is possible for a community to be forged simply because one is necessary.

The overarching approach is that of dialectics—an emphasis on the contradictions or tensions inherent in everyday life. Perhaps the most basic tension, one that has been noted by other commentators on American communal life, is that between the individual and the social group, between personal wants and institutional prerogatives. The communication process both reflects awareness of this tension (as well as others) and is the route to a resolution, albeit a tentative and fragile one.

The results of Adelman and Frey's study of communal tensions and resolutions are not merely academic, but are designed to be useful to residents and administrators at the facility as well. Indeed, the book provides valuable insights for residents and administrators of comparable facilities who are struggling with issues of community building. Readers are presented with both observational and attitudinal data on the journey that residents take as they enter a place like Bonaventure House and build a life together.

What, then, is the role of communication in creating a viable community from what begins as a group of quite separate individuals? Members of a community share a common set of meanings. These meanings are created and maintained through specific communication practices, to which newcomers are oriented, that shape the social dynamics of everyday life, and that help residents cope as they see themselves and others become physically weak or die. These meanings permit community members to live together and coordinate their actions relating to a wide range of functions, from creating a schedule for taking turns washing dishes, to creating a new ritual for coping with and acknowledging death.

Thus, it is the potent, yet continuous, act of social creation despite participants' weakening physical bodies that Adelman and Frey seek to document. We learn that social stability, if viewed as an ongoing process, can be created in the context of extreme physical fragility and external social–political pressures. We are left to ponder whether the fact that it can be created at Bonaventure House means that it can be created elsewhere, too.

—*Wendy Leeds-Hurwitz*
—*Stuart J. Sigman*

Acknowledgments

This book is the culmination of years of supportive relationships in which colleagues, students, friends, and the people of Bonaventure House contributed insights, listened to ideas, and encouraged our work.

We would like to thank our respective universities. Mara would like to thank the Seattle University College of Arts and Sciences and the Seattle University Faculty Fellowship Awards for their support. She expresses a special thank you to her department faculty—Gary Atkins, Tomas Guillen, and Jeff Philpott—for their warm collegiality throughout this project. Larry would like to thank his colleagues at Loyola University Chicago, especially W. Barnett Pearce and Bren Murphy, for their support of this work over many years.

We offer a humble "thank you" to Shawny Anderson, colleague and friend, whose close reading and conscientious feedback was truly a gift. We appreciate the support of our editors, Wendy Leeds-Hurwitz and Stuart Sigman, and Larry Hayden IV and Kathleen O'Malley at Lawrence Erlbaum Associates. We also want to thank Jim Query, Loyola University Chicago, and Lyle Flint, Ball State University, for assistance in analyzing our survey data. Several students were integral to this project and their assistance is deeply appreciated: Mary Ann Wright, Kelly Michaud, and Jessica Harris.

As to our respective personal communities, Mara would like to thank Dwight Conquergood, Thomas Farrell, and Tamar Katriel, who have always encouraged fieldwork at the margins. Larry would like to thank Stephen Hartnett for his enthusiastic support, and Marni Cameron, whose love and understanding teach the meaning of connection. We both wish to thank Gary and Stephanie Kreps, whose friendship initiated and sustained our coauthorship.

This work is a collaboration with the Alexian Brothers of America and the staff and residents of Bonaventure House. We wish to convey our profound respect to Brother Felix Bettendorf for his leadership in guiding the Alexian vision in establishing Bonaventure House, and Timothy J. Budz, MSW, Executive Director of Bonaventure House, who gave generously of his time and energy in facilitating this study over the years. We also want to thank Paul Merideth, who volunteers his professional services as a photographer to Bonaventure House, and shared his poignant images of the house with us.

Ethnographic research often cites a key informant who helps guide the study. This term doesn't begin to capture the friendship, support, and personal insights that Fela has shared with us. Throughout the years, she has remained our anchor.

Most important, this book would not be possible without the trust and friendship of so many residents of Bonaventure House. As we listen to the tapes of our interviews, we are reminded of the devastation of AIDS; so many of those who shared their hopes, dreams, and pain with us have passed on. We are truly grateful for their trust in us.

❋ ❋ ❋ ❋ ❋ ❋ ❋ ❋ ❋

SPECIAL DEDICATION

They say that there are only six degrees of separation between everyone on the planet; that we are only six people away from being related to someone who died of AIDS. For Larry, the distance is much shorter. This book is dedicated to Glenn Stapelman, the cousin I wish I had known better, and now will never have the chance.

1

The Search For Community

Our yearning for community has been both eulogized and canonized. Hillary Clinton, in a speech about the greatest crisis in the United States, referred to the absence and profound need for community as "the sleeping sickness of the soul" (Quindlen, 1993, p. 17). From neighborhood watch groups to grand rhetorical appeals for sustaining national cohesion, the reclamation of community is heralded as the panacea for what ails us. When used in this way as a "god term," community is supposed to lead us to utopia, the promised land "in which humankind's deepest yearnings, noblest dreams, and highest aspirations come to fulfillment, where all physical, social, and spiritual forces work together, in harmony, to permit the attainment of everything people find necessary and desirable" (Kanter, 1972, p. 1).

Longing for community is particularly poignant in "the postmodern era," the abstract label that describes the fragmented chaos of our lives. We are beset with no sense of place (Meyrowitz, 1985), a saturated self (Gergen, 1991), and an inability to conceive of the public good (Bellah, Madsen, Sullivan, Swidler, & Tipton, 1985, 1991). The forces of urbanization, industrialization, and technology, especially the mass media, are said to make it virtually impossible for people to connect meaningfully with others. In such a world, community bespeaks what we have lost and are trying to regain.

Perhaps our desire for community is a reaction to the discourse of individualism that historically has dominated our collective psyche. de Tocqueville's (1841/1969) observations in the 19th century portrayed social life in the United States as one of rugged individualism that made collective action difficult: "Individualism is a calm and considered feeling which predisposes each citizen to isolate himself from the mass of his fellows and withdraw into the circle of family and friends; with this little society formed to his taste, he gladly leaves the greater society to look after itself" (p. 506).

Privileging individualism at the expense of community is still a dominant theme in the United States. Even the ability to talk about community is overshadowed by the hegemonic discourse of individualism. As Gergen (1991) claimed:

> [T]he Western vocabulary of understanding persons is robustly individualistic. The culture has long been committed to the idea of the single, conscious self as the critical unit of society. . . . Private consciousness marks both the beginning and ending of our lives. Thus we stand at the present historical juncture with a massive array of terms to depict the individual. . . . In contrast, we have an impoverished language of relatedness. (p. 160)

In spite of the ideology of individualism, or perhaps more likely as a result of it, there is deep respect for community in the United States. From a dialectical perspective, the individual and the collective are two sides of the same coin—one simply cannot exist without the other. It is not surprising, therefore, that fascination with individualism in the United States is accompanied by the aggressive search for community. de Tocqueville, himself, was astounded that, in the face of such individualism, the United States was a country of joiners, where social connections abounded in voluntary associations. Columnist George Will (cited in Shaffer & Anundsen, 1993) contended, "Clearly this nation, though steeped in the severe individualism of the frontier notion of freedom, has a yearning for the community feeling that comes from collective undertakings. ...The question is whether any enterprise other than war can tap that yearning" (p. 4).

The communities of yesteryear, however, were insulated groups based on ethnic, religious, and/or racial similarity, that defined themselves in opposition to other groups, and supported members only if they followed strict rules of conduct. As Shaffer and Anundsen (1993) explained:

> As tightly knit and stable as most old-style communities were, they were also homogeneous, suspicious of outsiders, socially and economically stratified, emotionally stifling, and limited in opportunities for personal and professional development. So long as members belonged to the right ethnic, religious, or racial groups—or stayed in their place if they did not—and behaved within a narrowly defined set of parameters, they could count on strong communal support. But if they strayed too far outside the lines, their fellow community members might well shun or harass them. (p. 6)

These communities can still be found today; indeed, Bellah et al. (1985), in their widely acclaimed study of U.S. values and mores, argued that contemporary social life has been reduced to "lifestyle enclaves" with minimal social interdependence. However, new and diverse social configurations, based not on blood ties but on common concerns and issues, are emerging. They take the form of support groups, residential settings, speech communities, and even a small, but respectable, political movement known as communitarianism that is dedicated "to creating a new moral, social, and public order based on restored communities, without allowing puritanism or oppression" (Etzioni, 1993, p. 2). Even more ephemeral, the quest for connectedness is found in the "network communities" of disembodied cyberspace, where "people in virtual communities do just about everything people do in real life, but we leave our bodies behind" (Rheingold, 1993, p. 3).

Americans hunger for these new-style communities. Consider, for example, their participation in support groups, from 12-step recovery programs to women's groups to Bible study groups. In a national, representative survey of the U.S. public, Wuthnow (1994) reported that 4 of every 10 adults belong to a small group of relative strangers who meet regularly to provide caring and support for one another. Although there are critics of this transient form of connection (e.g., Kaminer, 1992; Parks, 1995), there can be little doubt that "the small-group movement has been effecting a quiet revolution in American society . . . both providing community and changing our understanding of what community is" (Wuthnow, 1994, pp. 2, 11).

What is this compelling concept of "community" that inspires such passions and quests? The purpose of this work is to understand the profound need for community by focusing on how communicative practices help create and sustain everyday communal life amidst the crises of human loss. We explore these ideas within a particular type of new-style community—a residential setting for persons with AIDS, where the web of social relationships and the demands of a life-threatening illness intersect in complex ways. Facing a life-threatening illness can defy meaningful social connections, but it can also inspire such ties, sometimes in ways that elude us in the course of daily life. If we understand how collective communicative practices help residents forge a sense of community out of the fragility and chaos of living together with AIDS, perhaps we may learn something about forging community in our relatively stable environments.

Prior to opening the door and entering this residential facility, we briefly examine the elusive, but seemingly intuitive, concept of community. We certainly do not intend to reinvent the wheel; instead, we offer this discussion as a way of specifying the boundary conditions that inform the study of community reported in this book. After providing a condensed version of the physical, emotional, and societal impact of AIDS, we present a brief history of Bonaventure House, one of the largest residences for persons with AIDS in the United States. We conclude this chapter with a discussion of our methodological commitments and approach to studying communication and community in this setting.

COMMUNICATION AND COMMUNITY

One way community is traditionally defined is with respect to space, whether local neighborhoods or virtual space over the Internet. "In ordinary speech for most people in the U.S., the term community refers to people with whom I identify in a locale" (I. M. Young, 1995, p. 244). We too are interested in space, but our view is that "place attachment," the emotional bonding of people and groups to places and things (Altman & Low, 1992), is constructed via their relational connections with others who share that space. As Hawley (1984) noted, "Virtually all of our experience with the physical environment is filtered through the social environment" (p. 6). A person only speaks fondly of a town, after all, if he or she has positive relational experiences while living there. The physical environment is fundamentally:

> [a] context, milieu, or setting in which relationships are embedded. So, for example, homes and dwellings reflect the importance of physical places to personal relationships, a point made salient in the case of so-called "homeless" people, who might just as easily be called "workless" people. But the term "homelessness" reflects more than the loss of a job; it acknowledges the loss of a crucial place where pragmatic, relational, and symbolic events and indicators of being a whole person and integral family are carried out. (Altman, 1993, p. 32)

In their work on the psychological sense of community, McMillan and Chavis (1986) referenced community with regard to emotional connections between people who mutually feel a sense of belonging to a particular group in a particular space. Scholars generally agree that community is "a kind of interpersonal unity that is somehow authentic as distinguished from various kinds of interpersonal unity that are merely apparent" (Tinder, 1995, p. 66). Authentic interpersonal connection is "invested with all the sentiment attached to kinship, friendship, [and] neighbouring" (Cohen, 1985, p. 13).

Emotional connection is a choice community members make that reaffirms their humanness, in addition to providing material and/ or psychological safety and security. In her work on intentional communities, such as communes, Kanter (1972) noted:

> The search for community is also a quest for direction and purpose in a collective anchoring of the individual life. Investment of self in a community, acceptance of its authority and willingness to support its values, is dependent in part on the extent to which group life can offer identity, personal meaning, and the opportunity to grow in terms of standards and guiding principles that the member feels are expressive of his own inner being. (p. 73)

Emotional connection creates and, in turn, is created by shared individual and collective beliefs, values, and attitudes about community life and a common set of customs, activities, and communicative patterns in which members engage. What ties people together in a community is a common way of viewing themselves and others. Community is thus a "common symbol system" in which members create and maintain a shared set of meanings. "The reality of community in people's experience thus inheres in their attachment or commitment to a common body of symbols" (Cohen, 1985, p. 16), leading to what Hunter (1974) called a *symbolic community*.

This shared culture inevitably is expressed in structural features of community life. Kanter (1968) argued that control, whereby members agree to abide by common rules, is an inherent feature of community life, and McMillan and Chavis (1986) spoke of community members influencing one another's behavior. Communities are social systems with distinctive rules, norms, patterns of social interaction, and social control (Jeffres, Dobos, & Sweeney, 1987).

Thus, to use Geertz's (1973) famous metaphor for culture, community is a *web* spun of space, identity, emotional connection, interdependence, common symbols, and mutual influence. The spinning of this web is what interests us most in this text, for we believe that community is constituted (created) and reconstituted (sustained) in communicative practices. Rothenbuhler (1991) claimed that "communication and community grow in each other's shadows; the possibilities of one are structured by the possibilities of the other" (p. 76). Community is both created and sustained by everyday patterns of human interaction (spinning the web) that take on shared meanings among the members of a particular group. "Abstract ideals of brotherhood and harmony, of love and union," noted Kanter (1972), "must be translated into concrete social practices" (p. 75). Even attempts to define a boundary that "encapsulates the identity of the community . . . are themselves largely constituted by people in interaction" (Cohen, 1985, p. 13). Ultimately, community is a social construction, grounded in the symbolic meanings and communicative practices of individuals, that fosters meaningful human interdependence in social aggregates.

Communication, therefore, is not just a variable contained within a community; community itself is best regarded as a phenomenon that emerges from communication. "Community, it may be said, is that which is realized in the activity of communication" (Tinder, 1995, p. 68). Communication is thus the essential, defining feature—the medium—of community. Conquergood's (1994) words about the making of culture also ring true for the making of community: "Communication practices of 'real live human beings' become the crucible of culture—the generative site where culture gets made and re-made" (p. 25).

LIVING WITH AIDS

We have chosen to study the connection between communication and community in a residential facility for people with AIDS (PWAs). Considering the physical devastation, uncertain symptomology, and omnipresent sense of impending death associated with this disease; the loss of significant others to AIDS and the fragile social networks left behind for those still living with it; and the societal stigma associated with AIDS that often results in the loss of social support; no other group of people may have more need for community than those affected by AIDS. It is not only the marginality, but the fragility of everyday life of PWAs that makes the creating and sustaining of community so compelling in this particular context.

This fragility, first of all, is due to the very real physical symptoms with which PWAs must contend. AIDS, however it is defined by governmental proclamation, results from the attack of the HIV virus on the immune system. AIDS, consequently, is a syndrome of complex disorders that results from an increasingly weakened immune system (referred to technically as "depressed immune competence"). Depending on the body's response, there is a wide range of possible symptoms, including candidiasis (fungus, also called thrush), Kaposi's sarcoma (cancer of skin and tissue), pelvic inflammatory disease, tuberculosis (TB), and dementia (mental deterioration). R. J. Miller (1991) summarized the clinical challenge in caring for PWAs:

> That AIDS patients and their families require more intensive level of support services . . . [than] traditional hospice patients is well known. These patients are relatively young. Many present pain control difficulty because of a long-standing history of drug abuse. More than half of them have severe and persistent diarrheas. Others have progressive dementia and blindness. (p. 9)

Perhaps what is most disturbing for PWAs is the uncertain timing and ambiguity of the physical symptoms of AIDS. "Unpredictability and uncontrollability result in a disjunction between the person and the body. . . . The body becomes an 'other'—at best an unpredictable ally" (Freund & McGuire, 1995, p. 145). Is it a harmless cough or the sign of a life-threatening lung infection?

AIDS can also be a physically dehumanizing affliction. Imagine how hard it is to feel dignified when forced to wear diapers due to lack of bowel control. Loss of physical control, so valued in society, can have devastating consequences:

> People experience an assault on their sense of self when their illness involves loss of control, such as incontinence, loss of bowel control, flatulence, seizures, stumbling and falls, tics and tremors, and drooling. We rely on relative control of our bodies to present ourselves in socially valued ways (Goffman, 1963; Schneider & Conrad, 1983), but chronic illness and disability disrupt that control. (Freund & McGuire, 1995, p. 147)

The physical problems associated with AIDS can produce severe psychological changes that result in an involuntary redefinition of self, symbolic crises of self-identity (Query, 1987), such as redefining one's self in relationship to one's past and future, and heightened self-consciousness (Charmaz, 1987, 1991).

The physical and psychological problems associated with AIDS are compounded by the social devastation and loss that accompany this disease. No other illness in recent memory in the United States has resulted in mourners who grieve not only for the loss of their friends, family, and lovers, but also for their own lives. Whole social networks, especially in gay communities, have been decimated.

There is also the highly charged social and political context in which this illness is embedded. Watney (1994), a noted critic of the cultural representation of HIV/AIDS education and media coverage, argued that the moral panic that accompanies the evolution of this disease is unprecedented; the public response to AIDS has become "a powerful condenser for a great range of social, sexual and psychic anxieties" (p. 9). Watney noted:

> We are not living through a distinct, coherent "moral panic" concerning AIDS, a panic with a linear narrative and the prospect of closure. On the contrary, we are witnessing the ideological manoeuvres which unconsciously "make sense" of this accidental triangulation of disease, sexuality, and homophobia. (p. 11)

So powerful are the associations and symbolic triggers of this illness that Sontag (1989) argued that AIDS has become *the* contemporary societal metaphor for chaos and paranoia. The discourses of pollution, plague, deviance, sin, and punishment/poetic justice (e.g., "the wrath of God") invoked so commonly to reference AIDS (see Lupton, 1993, 1994; Patton, 1990; Redman, 1991; Ross, 1989) powerfully shape people's perceptions (see Norton, Schwartzbaum, & Wheat, 1990). AIDS has become the "very face of contagion of our time" (Brandt, 1985, p. 194) that exposes "the hidden vulnerabilities in the human condition" (Fineberg, 1988, p. 128). In the process, AIDS literally and symbolically has refigured social reality (see Gagnon, 1989, 1992; Herdt, 1992), be this in homophobic political rhetoric or the new abstinence-based sex education curriculum.

Much has been written about the stigma associated with a disease where public obsession with distinctions between "innocent" and "guilty" victims has created a two-tier system of the afflicted (see E. Albert, 1986; Treichler, 1987), where labeling risk groups (vs. risk behaviors) results in a transformation of a disease into a *malade imaginaire* (Watney, 1994), and where the stigma becomes a marker for unemployment and social isolation. AIDS "moves along the fault lines of society and becomes a metaphor for understanding that society" (Bateson & Goldsby, 1988, p. 2), serving as a social X ray of who is acceptable and who is not (Carrier & Magaña, 1992; Gagnon, 1989). Ryan White, the young boy with AIDS who crusaded for social acceptance in the public schools, captured the public's sympathy, but such media campaigns have not been extended as readily to minorities, intravenous drug users, or even mothers with AIDS.

Crandall and Coleman (1992) identified two main sources of the stigmatization of PWAs: the fear of deadly contagion of the illness itself, and the fact that the majority of those with the disease, at least in the United States, come from already stigmatized groups—homosexuals, bisexuals, and intravenous drug users. Members of these stigmatized groups who have AIDS thus bear a double scarlet letter, potentially casting them beyond society's margins.

It is not surprising, therefore, that emotional reactions by members of mainstream society toward PWAs are often highly negative (see Cawyer & Smith-Dupré, 1995). As Suczek and Fagerhaugh (1991) maintained, some individuals view "any contact with a person with AIDS as tantamount to a death sentence" (p. 164). Even doctors and nurses sometimes respond irrationally to HIV/AIDS patients (see Klonoff & Ewers, 1990; Norton et al., 1990).

Clearly, PWAs are in need of a tremendous amount of social support. As Adelman (1989) contended:

> Few persons with AIDS will be immune to the emotional devastation and uncertainty that accompany the uncontrollable course of this illness. For such persons there is little doubt that a major resource for coping will be the "healing web" (Pilisuk & Parks, 1986), the constellation of informal caregivers—community members, kin and lovers or friends who provide social support. (p. 31)

Many PWAs, however, are not receiving the social support they need. Sometimes this deficit occurs because they, like other stigmatized people, withdraw from interactions, cutting off usual sources of social support (see Cline & Boyd, 1993; Kleck, 1968; Scheerhorn, 1990). More frequently, decreases in support are linked to the collapse of social networks. Too often, PWAs are faced with "hostility and ostracism rather than support" (Cleveland, 1987, p. 3). AIDS, unfortunately, is an illness so imbued with fear and contempt that even loving family members are afraid to visit their dying sons and daughters.

The disintegration of traditional support systems has led many PWAs to turn to each other for social support. Social services and support groups for PWAs, such as the Body Positive, Test Positive Aware, and the Brigade in San Francisco, serve as models of mutual support (see Crandall & Coleman, 1992; Gordon & Pavlis, 1989).

PWAs, however, often need more than support groups; many need physical shelter. Hospitals are usually ill-equipped to handle the nonacute needs of PWAs, whereas nursing homes often refuse to provide them with palliative care. Loss of housing affects a "disproportionate number of people who are HIV positive or who have AIDS" (Schietinger, 1988, p. 481). Indeed, the overall housing picture for PWAs is both distressing and depressing, as the demand far exceeds the number of available alternatives, resulting in a new generation of homeless people. In New York City alone, for example, estimates place the number of homeless people with AIDS as high as 13,000, yet there are fewer than 500 rooms available expressly for PWAs (C. Brown, 1992). Even those with AIDS who can afford housing are in danger of becoming homeless due to discrimination, despite laws against such practices. And, as AIDS moves deeper into the poorer segments of society and shifts from a terminal illness to a chronic, life-threatening prognosis, the needs for adequate housing and hospice care are increasing dramatically.

Fortunately, despite this bleak picture, the response to AIDS has, from its very beginnings, been a grassroots movement that is synonymous with community (e.g., community education, caregiving, lobbying), and nowhere is this better illustrated than in community housing for PWAs. Innovative residential care facilities—called homes, hospices, and independent group living—sponsored by grassroots and/or religious groups provide an important source of physical and emotional support for PWAs, adding a radical voice that has redefined and reclaimed health care from traditional medical institutions. One of the residential facilities that pioneers a new model for the care of people with AIDS is Bonaventure House.

BONAVENTURE HOUSE:
THE FRAGILE COMMUNITY

"The pilgrim must embark within a shippe the Bonaventure named"
Nicholas Breton, 1592

In 1865, Brother Bonaventure embarked from his native Germany for an un-known future in a New World. He carried with him faith in God's goodness, a commitment to the healing ministry of Jesus, and a vision of an American Province of Alexian Brothers. In creating the Brothers' first hospital in Chicago and receiving there the first patients and the first American novices, he found his *Bonaventure*, his "good fortune," the fulfillment of his mission. Bonaventure House is an extension of the vision of Brother Bonaventure, our American Founder. Those who come to the house "the Bonaventure named" are welcomed as contemporary pilgrims in the name of Jesus, and in the open-hearted and caring spirit of Brother Bonaventure.

(Inscription on a plaque dedicated by Joseph Cardinal Bernadin, April 6, 1989, located in the lobby of Bonaventure House)

In response to the health crisis posed by AIDS and the need for housing for indigents with the disease, the Alexian Brothers of America founded Bonaventure House (BH), a residential facility for PWAs (see Fig. 1.1). Its conception was grounded in the order's European origins in the 14th century, where the Brothers cared for the sick during the plague.

In 1866, Brother Bonaventure opened the first U.S. hospital of the Alexian Brothers in Chicago. In those days, Chicago was a hotbed of diseases—scarlet fever, smallpox, dysentery, whooping cough, and measles, to name a few. It was the outbreak of cholera, however, that "provided Brother Bonaventure and the Alexian Brothers in Chicago their baptism of fire" (Davidson, 1990, p. 13). A second hospital was soon built, and the Alexian Brothers' health care ministry in Chicago was firmly established.

Although theirs is not a radical or politically motivated order, the Brothers have taken clear moral stands and set new precedents for health care. Early in the 1950s, for example, their "ministry of healing" eliminated segregated Negro wards, and adopted a nondiscriminatory policy in hiring Black doctors and enrolling Black students in their nursing school (Davidson, 1990). Brother Felix Bettendorf (1993), President of the Alexian Brothers Health System, noted, "the Alexian Charism Statement [their mission statement] explicitly challenges

FIG. 1.1. Located in an established, upscale neighborhood on the north side of
Chicago, Bonaventure House is a residential facility for people with AIDS
(photograph by Paul Merideth).

the Brothers to reach out 'to the poor, sick and dying, especially the marginated and powerless'" (p. 5). For the Alexian Brothers, BH represents the roots of their mission (see Fig. 1.2).

Guided by the Alexian Spirit of compassion and dignity for all, the Alexian Brothers Bonaventure House is an organization whose purpose is to enhance the quality of life for people living with HIV infection. Bonaventure House offers people the opportunity for assisted living within a comprehensive supportive environment. Bonaventure House offers services which support and maintain the dignity of those being served without regard to race, gender, sexual orientation, religious beliefs, physical challenges or income.

FIG. 1.2.   1996 Bonaventure House Mission Statement.

The Brothers invested $1.4 million to start the house. They selected an established, upscale neighborhood located on the north side of Chicago, rather than an isolated setting, because of easy access to medical facilities (BH is located across the street from a hospital) and to prevent further marginalization of people with AIDS. As a result of this decision, they encountered the expected powerful opposition from neighborhood and local community groups, who cried "not in my backyard." At the end of 2 years of fighting, $40,000 in legal fees, and a bitter all-day hearing before the Zoning Board of the City of Chicago, they finally were granted a permit. On March 22, 1989, BH opened its doors to 26 residents, and later expanded to accommodate 30 residents.

Early BH demographics portrayed a predominately White, male, homosexual resident population. However, as AIDS moved deeper into other populations, BH began to reflect a wider cross section of the population affected by it. By 1993, the people of Bonaventure House were "men and women, people of color and white people, rich and poor, homosexual and heterosexual, famous and infamous, religious and irreligious, young and old, the healthy, the HIV-infected and those who themselves live each day with AIDS" (S. J. Miller, Ward, & Rybicki, 1993, p. 13; see Fig. 1.3).

As of November 1995, BH has housed 274 residents: (a) 248 men and 26 women; (b) 136 Caucasians, 105 African Americans, 26 Hispanics, and 7 others; and (c) 199 homosexuals and 77 heterosexuals. The average age range is between 30–39, but there have been residents as young as 20 and as old as 69, some of whom are parents with young or grown children. Fifty to sixty percent of the residents have a history of alcohol or drug abuse, and approximately 25% contracted HIV through intravenous drug usage. The average length of stay is 233 days, just over 7 months. Regrettably, 195, over 71%, of the residents have died since the house opened.

Unlike a hospice, which serves those in the final stages of the death and dying process, BH is designed to foster assisted living to ambulatory PWAs. In the words of one of the Brothers, the Alexians wanted "more than a place to park one's shoes at night"; they wanted a home that would foster physical, emo-

FIG. 1.3.   The residents and staff of Bonaventure House, as shown in this 1994
photograph, reflect a wide cross section of the population (photograph by Paul Merideth).

tional, and spiritual well-being. Modeled after their own contemplative living
experience, the Alexian Brothers worked with the architect to design a house
that ensured small, private living quarters for each resident (every two residents
share a bathroom; their partner is referred to humorously as their "johnnymate"), semiprivate social space, and large public rooms for daily communal
meals and leisure. There is a chapel in the house, along with administrative
offices, an internal courtyard, and a separate parking lot.

BH costs more than $1 million a year to operate. Financial support is obtained
through federal agencies, religious groups, philanthropic institutions and busi-
nesses, individual donors, and rent paid by residents who work (45% of their
income). The day-to-day operations of the house are managed by an Executive
Director who handles four basic functions: administration and budgeting; staffing;
long-range planning; and development/funding. Thirteen full-time and 14 part-
time staff members provide 24-hour supervision, medical and nursing care, case
management (see Budz, 1993), an array of social services, pastoral care (see

DiDomenico, 1993), house maintenance, and food preparation. There are also more than 150 volunteers, whose responsibilities include house maintenance, some administrative duties (e.g., answering the phone), and, most important, offering social support to residents. Due to zoning restrictions, BH staff and volunteers cannot administer hands-on medical care. Nursing and hospice personnel, therefore, are engaged as needed (see Van Loon, 1993).

Residents' responsibilities include maintenance of their room and rotating dish duty, which, as discussed in chapter 3, becomes a contested practice for house members. Attendance at weekly house meetings is mandatory, as it is for weekly support groups during the first 6 weeks of residency (thereafter, it is voluntary) and weekly support groups for those recovering from alcohol and other drug abuse throughout their stay at BH (see Boyle, 1993). Voluntary conjoint activities include spiritual services and social/entertainment events, such as video nights, parties, and field trips.

Our text tries to show how collective communicative practices help residents forge a sense of community out of the chaos of living together with AIDS. But before we explore these practices, we describe how we came to BH and our commitments to both research and residents. In particular, we discuss how a dialectical perspective offers a rich and helpful way to understand the inherent pushes and pulls of community life. For community and chaos are not a duality; they are, indeed, a dialectic.

STUDYING COMMUNICATION
AND COMMUNITY AT BONAVENTURE HOUSE:
THE DIALECTICAL PERSPECTIVE

Detached descriptions of "site access" do not convey the more organic, emergent way in which our interest in BH began. Mara lived only a block away from the house, and became involved as a volunteer shortly after it opened, with no intentions of conducting research. She recalls in her own voice her early days at BH:

Apart from my weekly volunteer time, residents knew me as "The Video Queen," renting videos and watching them with residents, occasionally cooking a meal, and hanging out at the house on weekends. In truth, BH was like my second home. When I was approached by the administration to conduct a study of residents' experiences, I declined at first, unwilling to redefine my role from "insider" (volunteer) to "outsider" (researcher). However, it was hard to resist this carte blanche invitation to design an independent research program in a confidential, private setting usually off-limits to outsiders. But it was more than researcher greed that motivated this investigation. I was deeply moved by the precariousness of social life—indeed, life itself—and the richness of formal and informal communication that provided stability amidst fragility.

Ironically, the shift from volunteer to researcher was more problematic for the administration than for residents or for me. The professional client–worker relationship adopted by BH administrators places inordinate emphasis on professional boundaries, defined operationally by job titles, task descriptions, and type of involvement with residents. Due to confusion regarding the distinction between contract research (ownership by the funding agency) and independent academic research (ownership by the researcher), legal discussions of the formal agreement about the research entailed a few heated meetings over ownership of the data, editorial control, and copyright of written reports. I argued that these had to stay within my domain, to ensure both adherence to the protocols agreed on with the Human Subjects Review Board at my university, and academic freedom in final publications. Agreements were finally reached, and collaboration with the agency required administrators' input into the research design, a 2-week editorial review of manuscripts to be submitted for publication (in which their reactions and suggestions would be considered and, if rejected, they could decide to keep the name of the house anonymous), and an oral and written report to both staff and residents on the research findings.

In part, the tensions in the research negotiations resulted in suspending my participation as a volunteer, which the administration contended would create a role conflict for residents. This was a serious problem for ethnographic research and almost jeopardized the study. Emotionally, I was unwilling to sacrifice my relationships with residents to become a sequestered interloper. However, the restriction proved less of a deterrent to active participation than imagined. Although my official transition from volunteer to researcher was announced formally during a house meeting, the role shift was rather seamless. Although I was not actively engaged in volunteering, prolonged visits for interviews still enabled personal involvement with residents.

In early 1990, I interviewed 21 residents about various aspects of communicative practices and community life at BH. After the results of this initial study were presented, the administration determined that this cross-sectional study did not capture residents' ongoing experiences sufficiently. Hence, I offered to conduct a series of interviews and questionnaires over a 3-year period.

It was at this time, fall of 1991, that Larry joined the project. He, too, recalls in his own voice this collaboration:

Mara and I had been friends for some years, and had talked a great deal about her involvement with Bonaventure House. I had the greatest respect for her personal and professional commitments to this house.

Mara and I had always wanted to work together, because my focus on applied group communication complemented her expertise on social support, but our various commitments had prevented collaboration. After the summer of 1991, when Mara was designing the longitudinal research project at BH, my work schedule freed up and we decided to collaborate.

Although Mara and I had talked much about AIDS and about BH, I must admit to being rather naive, approaching this initially as a research project. This seemed fine at first, for we decided that I would remain somewhat at a distance from the house as an "outside" researcher, whereas Mara's ethnographic researcher role put her "inside" the house. In the spring of 1993, however, Mara moved overseas, and then relocated to Seattle in August 1994. This move came at a good time for me, for I had formed emotional attachments to the people of BH, and had already decided to give up the researcher role and become a volunteer, which I still am today.

Our research is thus a unique collaboration in which one of us is "inside" the house and the other remains "outside" it. This etic–emic relationship proved invaluable for engaging in "subjective versus objective" dialogues (some might call them fights) about research design, interpretation of results, and written and oral reports. This relationship also provided a powerful coping mechanism, as the emotional toll of this study cannot be underestimated. AIDS exacts its own human costs on those who do ethnographic research (Quimby, 1992), and we know those costs only too well. Bereavement over the continual loss of residents to whom we became close, and pain in hearing their voices (via audio and videotape) long after their deaths, resulted in much grieving and distress during our research discussions. We know it is easy to become emotionally drained by this research, and the support we provided one another helped us continue our work in the face of such difficulties.

People living together with AIDS are pilgrims embarking on a frightening journey about which little is known and much is unpredictable. We too embarked on this project with no prepackaged plan. We often treaded water, looking for ways to make sense of what was happening, exacerbated, no doubt, by our multiple roles as researchers, volunteers, and friends of residents.

Our research procedures reflect a commitment to what Lincoln and Guba (1985) called the *naturalistic paradigm*. Proponents of this paradigm believe that the goal of research is to "reconstruct the 'world' at the only place at which it exists: in the minds of constructors" (Guba, 1992, p. 27). Methodologically, this reconstruction employs hermeneutics and dialectics. "The hermeneutic aspect consists in depicting individual constructions as accurately as possible, while the dialectical aspect consists of comparing and contrasting these existing individual (including the inquirer's) constructions" (Guba, 1992, p. 26).

A significant goal of this text, therefore, is to give voice to those whom we have been privileged to know throughout our research. One person with AIDS is quoted as saying, "Anthropologists of our tristes tropiques have accumulated a considerable store of information and conclusions about our genes and our mores, our model of socialization and our myths, but in so doing, they've lost sight of our humanity" (cited in Dreuilh, 1988, p. 4). We thus give primacy to residents' voices—believing that "any analysis not based on some translation of the symbols used by people of that culture is open to suspicion" (Wilson, 1957, p. 6)—and weave into the narrative our own and other researchers' voices. Residents are quoted verbatim (their names are changed, in some cases to pseudonyms they requested, to assure anonymity), as are staff (pseudonyms are used, except where permission has been given to use their full name), although occasionally their comments are edited for the sake of clarity. We strive to capture as fully as possible the ways residents, staff, and we as participant–observers, volunteers, and academicians make sense of life and death at BH.

To do so, we rely primarily on data obtained through participant observation and in-depth interviews with residents and staff. We formally interviewed a total of 43 residents at three different points in time, from 1991–1995, along with 11 full-time staff members. We also had many informal conversations with residents, staff, and volunteers.

Although an interview protocol was followed carefully (including initial discussion of the study, its purpose, overview of the interview, audiotaping, and permission forms signed), we were acutely aware that some of the issues raised could be stressful to residents. Contributing to research and leaving a legacy as motivations for sharing their story can be therapeutic and beneficial for residents. But we are also aware that getting "the juiciest quotes" can cause residents distress, especially in our discussions with them about death and dying. Knowing that researcher greed is tempting, easy to rationalize, and, at times, difficult to avoid, we attempted to abide by the edict "to do no harm," and, hence, movement toward more invasive and painful discussion during these interviews proceeded in careful, incremental steps.

The term *interviews* does not really capture these interactions well, for these conversations are part of an ongoing relationship with residents and, in many cases, are filled with profound emotions shared by both parties. Marcus and Fischer (1986) contended that the underlying metaphor for ethnography is dialogue, and that is what we seek to establish in our discussions with residents and staff. As Geist and Dreyer (1993) explained:

> The dialogic lens includes the researcher not just as an observer of the discourse. ... Taking the dialogic perspective to heart challenges researchers to communicate with research participants in ways that overcome the asymmetry that often undermines the participants' experience and understanding. Dialogic interviewing's primary goal is to empower respondents by engaging them in dialogue. (p. 245)

Our years of participant observation and extensive interviews also provided us with a basis for constructing and administering a questionnaire. This questionnaire explored many features of community life at BH, from participation in collective communicative practices to metaphors residents and staff use to characterize the house. The survey questions emerged from a combination of residents' concerns and issues raised during previous interviews, questions administrators wanted answered, and our concerns as communication researchers. We administered this questionnaire to residents and staff at four different times (March 1993; August 1993; September 1994; and April 1995). In total, 59 residents and 27 staff members completed at least one questionnaire. We provide descriptive information from these questionnaires when appropriate (using the first questionnaire participants completed).

Our research practices thus relied on participatory methods, and we attempted to follow three general guidelines Frey (1994) outlined for such research: research as a partnership, as a tool for social action, and as sustained interaction between researchers and those they study. Accordingly, this text is part of a larger body of work that reflects our collaborative relationship with the members of BH. For example, the concepts and models discussed in our written reports are used by administrators to help new staff and volunteers understand BH. At the request of administrators, we also wrote a chapter in a handbook for assisted living produced by BH (Frey & Adelman, 1993), and coauthored an article for health care administrators with the Executive Director of BH (Adelman, Frey, & Budz, 1994). An ethnographic videotape about BH produced by Adelman and Schultz (1991) is used in training new volunteers and in fundraising efforts. Proceeds from the sale of this videotape go to the BH Residents' Fund and a fund for conducting more research on the house. Rough drafts of this text were given to key participants and their feedback was incorporated in the final version. In this spirit of partnership, our work strives to capture members' views of this community from their perspective, giving residents a voice, even after death.

Finally, unlike the study of insects pinned to a dissecting board, social life does not sit still for scrutiny. Alas, even when the researcher is content with a seemingly stable image of the subject, he or she must go beyond the obvious, and question the many alternative points of view. Murphy (1971) proposed using the *dialectical exercise*, arguing that a researcher should:

> Question everything that he sees and hears, examine phenomena fully and from every angle, seek and evaluate the contradiction of any proposition, and consider every category from the viewpoint of its noncontents as well as its positive attributes. It [the dialectical exercise] requires us to also look for paradox as much as complementarity, for opposition as much as accommodation. It portrays a universe of dissonance underlying apparent order and seeks deeper orders beyond the dissonance. (p. 117)

Clearly, the dialectical exercise is not a detached analytic perspective. In the ethnographic study of natural groups, the very process of study entails a dialectical experience for the researcher between, for example, emic and etic stances, subjectivity and objectivity, and experiences near and far. Herdt (1992) spoke to the personalized and dialectical experience in ethnographic studies of AIDS:

> The field-worker is, by historical definition, both insider and outsider, stranger and friend. We are usually known at the grass-roots level and our work reflects a deeper understanding [than traditional social scientists] of issues such as what is risk, how do PWAs live their lives, and what are their needs. (p. 16)

We took the dialectical exercise to heart, and now see a dialectical perspective as crucial for understanding both community in general and community at BH. Community life is like a tightrope, held taut by the sustained tensions of daily living. We believe that this metaphor, unlike more romanticized, stable images of community, captures the precarious collective structures and relationships that sustain group living. Human relationships are riddled with contradictions, inconsistencies, and paradoxes; fluctuations between regularity and change are thus more like a tightrope than a featherbed.

At the heart of dialectical analysis is the notion of tensions that need to be managed: "A dialectic is a tension between two or more contradictory elements in a system that demands at least temporary resolution" (Littlejohn, 1996, p. 265). Dialectical contradictions "are not merely different from one another or in conflict with one another; they are the underlying opposing tendencies in a phenomenon which mutually exclude and simultaneously presuppose one another" (Goldsmith, 1990, p. 538).

Many researchers have demonstrated the richness of a dialectical perspective for examining the tensions of relational life (see Altman, 1993; Altman, Vinsel, & Brown, 1981; Askham, 1976; Baxter, 1988, 1990; Baxter & Montgomery, 1996; Bochner, 1984; Cissna, Cox, & Bochner, 1990; Goldsmith, 1990; Masheter & Harris, 1986; Rawlins, 1983, 1989, 1992; Rychlak, 1976; Smith & Berg, 1987; Werner & Baxter, 1994; Wilmot, 1987). The dialectical perspective helps, in particular, to understand a central paradox that underlies community life: as Tillich (1952) claimed, everyone who joins a group wishes to be both *a part* of the group and *apart* from it. Even converts to ideologically driven forms of collective and monastic utopias, such as communes and convents, experience tension between personal needs and group demands (Kanter, 1972). In U.S. culture, this tension is heightened by the values placed on individualism, independence, autonomy, and privacy.

Dialectics thus "form the pulse of routine as well as volatile and transitional moments ... [and are] the fundamental properties of social life" (Rawlins, 1992, p. 7). The dialectical tensions of communal life, of course, demand temporary resolution if a community is to sustain itself over time. Dialectical analysis, therefore, "looks at the ways the system develops or changes, how it moves, in response to these tensions; and it looks at the strategic actions taken by a system to resolve dialectical tensions" (Littlejohn, 1996, p. 265). In addition to examining the processes of regularization and situational adjustment in social life, a dialectical perspective demands that researchers also consider the factor of indeterminancy, or fluctuating conditions, where "established rules, customs and symbolic frameworks exist, but they operate in the presence of areas of indeterminancy, or ambiguity, or uncertainty and manipulability" (Moore, 1975, p. 220). Structural determinism, with its categorical analysis of roles, structure, and function is useful, but not sufficient for understanding how BH residents deal with the sense of being suspended, caught betwixt and between the wellness and illness continuum. Structure may help impose some order, but it cannot dismiss the chaos, where life itself is unpredictable.

This text seeks to uncover some of the ongoing oppositional forces of community life at BH, and the ways in which communicative practices massage these tensions. At the individual and collective levels, these tensions are experienced within a brief period of time—as noted, the average length of residents' stay is a little more than 7 months. In that time, residents move from being a newcomer, to a community member, to someone the community remembers.

We thus embed the study of dialectics into our discussions about community life at BH to reflect this short, but crystalized life, starting with the day a new resident opens the door to the day he or she passes away. Chapter 2 begins by examining the entry process for newcomers, chapter 3 explores the mundane, yet pivotal, moments of daily life at BH, and chapter 4 describes the issues of and practices for coping with death and dying. In each of these chapters, we reveal the dialectical tensions that community members encounter and attempt to massage. We conclude with an epilogue about some lessons we have learned about community life—to tolerate the messy, even conflicting, social needs that make community liveable. But first, let us begin by entering BH through the front door as experienced by newcomers.

2

The Fragility of Place:
The Entry Experience

Portrait of Scott

Scott was admitted twice to BH, first in 1989, then in 1992. This interview occurred several months into his second stay, at which time he was well-respected among residents and held a leadership position in the house. An articulate and devoutly religious man, Scott spoke of the tremendous fear, guilt, and anger that had prevailed in his life, and his gratitude to BH for helping him cope with these feelings and providing needed shelter and care:

> I wound up [early 1989] in a mental institute. At that particular time, a social worker referred me here. She asked me how did I feel about being in a residence such as this. That was exactly what I needed because I had a lot of fear—fear of dying, fear of being alone in my apartment. I always kept an apartment, but I chose not to stay there. I would sleep on the street, because that way I didn't have to be alone. So I came here. After staying here, I guess about 7 or 8 months, my attitude changed. I no longer was dying of AIDS; I learned how to live with AIDS.
>
> So I went back to work and got my family back together, and we stayed on that track for maybe a couple years. A couple of different circumstances . . . I chose to return back to my old ways to rid myself of frustration, so I was back to the self-pity, the guilt, the anger. I didn't know how to diffuse those feelings, and, again, the only things I could find to pacify me were drugs and alcohol. I was on a suicide trip. I would eat like once a week and that would be like a hamburger or a hotdog. My diet consisted of nothing but alcohol . . . that's what my life was

about, 'til I wound up in the hospital again with PCP [viral pneumonia]. They were ready to read my last rites, and the doc said, "Hey, not yet." After the struggle of trying to choose which direction I wanted to go, I thought about BH and I realized how helpful they had been to me, so that was my second admission here. Since then, God has tremendously blessed my life each and every moment of every day.

Portrait of Edward, Phd

Edward is a gentle, soft-spoken, independent scholar, working on a book based on his dissertation. Prior to entering BH, a friend, who was not wealthy, generously offered to pay Edward's rent, because he liked living alone. But Edward "hated" the feeling of being a burden. His health was slowly deteriorating, and a recent fall made him realize that he needed to be around people who could help. The sense of finality in moving to BH, however, resulted in unexpected reactions:

> It [coming to BH] was final. It was sorta, if I took this step, it's going to be hard to get back, if ever, so that was rather daunting. I had no idea I would have this claustrophobic reaction to this small room. There was an orientation session, I did see one room, and I came to lunch once before. I mean, I really was trying to be friendly and helpful and adapt, and so forth, but once I moved in, I really had a [bad] first week and got sort of depressed. It seemed like it had lifted, it got better, but about 2 weeks later, it really came down on me. This nurse here suggested that I go into an in-patient [treatment program] because I was talking so much about suicide. I was thinking about it. I don't even know really what happened then; it was a sense of being trapped, of claustrophobia, of not being able to get out. . . . There was also a loss of an environment where I didn't have to think that much about AIDS. There was like a remorse; there was the furniture loss, there was the place loss, and there was the loss of privacy, too.

Salvation or despair—these bipolar reactions reflect the range of emotions that residents might experience on entering BH. No single profile can do justice to the ways that newcomers enter BH and the adjustments they must make. This chapter begins by examining some of the profound emotions and reactions of incoming residents. The diverse nature of both new and veteran residents pose considerable problems for adjusting to life at BH. In response to these challenges, we examine the formal institutional communicative practices as well as the informal communicative practices that help ease the precariousness of initial entry for both newcomers and veterans. The chapter concludes by returning to the individual newcomer, focusing on how he or she chooses to cope with community life.

HEAVEN OR HELL:
EXPECTATIONS OF GROUP LIVING

People admitted to BH must be officially diagnosed by a medical doctor as having AIDS. Criteria for admission reflect demands from funding sources (e.g., preference for people in recovery, financial need, minorities), but also covers those who, independent of a predesignated qualification, are in distress in coping with their illness and appear to be strong candidates for community living (see Fig. 2.1). Links to various agencies and the reputation of BH in the local community result in referrals from hospitals, hospices, social services, rehabilitation centers, religious groups, and even word-of-mouth advertising at street fairs and events. Residents arrive from diverse places, whether destitute and living on the streets, residing in transient hotels, living with relatives, or owning a plush apartment or house.

Expectations about moving in to BH reflect these differences, and are captured by the wide range of residents' images of the house prior to entry: "a roof over my head and food on the table"; "a place to die"; "a bunch of real sick people"; "a classy place"; "like a nursing home"; "a halfway house"; "a hospice"; "a place to call home"; "hell"; and "a blessing." These images reflect whether newcomers see BH as an opportunity for or a loss of a "better life."

For many left homeless, destitute, and isolated by AIDS, their images and expectations of BH speak of hopefulness, not only in sustaining their health, but in accepting the illness. A large part of this acceptance results from being among other PWAs and having the opportunity to "talk about *it*" or not having to "explain *it*." When asked what she had gained in moving to BH, Rhonda noted, "Life. When I moved in here, it made me feel like I belonged. You can talk about it [AIDS]. I wasn't able to talk about it, except with my mother, because I had a lot of shame. Now I can talk about it and nobody looks down." Jason, another resident, spoke of his relief at not having to explain the disease:

> At least you know everyone else around here has AIDS and is not afraid of you because you have AIDS. You don't have to explain to anyone, "We can be friends, but there's one thing about me that you have to know. I have AIDS. Can you deal with that?" You know [at BH] you're not going to be ostracized because of an illness. That and the financial considerations make it easier.

Vincent, who had spent 6 of the past 7 years in prison, found inspiration for living from an example set by Mario, a dying resident who befriended him during his early days at BH:

> Mario was one of the first people who welcomed me because I like to joke and be kinda silly. He saw that in me the first week I was here. We got to be pretty close. When he was deteriorating in his bed, I used to go and rent a movie, and sit with him now and then. I was scared to get attached to him because I knew he was dying, but I did. It was gratifying to know that I had known him. Being in that

Bonaventure House (BH) will admit residents without regard to race, gender, sexual orientation, religious beliefs, physical handicap or income. Potential residents must have a confirmed diagnosis of Acquired Immune Deficiency Syndrome (AIDS) as set by the Centers for Disease Control criteria. Priority will be given to applicants who, 1) have exhausted all personal resources (family, friends, independent living) in their search for quality housing in a supportive atmosphere or 2) are unable to locate quality housing due to financial limitations imposed by their AIDS-defining illness. At the time of application each applicant will be considered for residency based on the following criteria:

SPECIFIC ACCEPTANCE GUIDELINES FOR ADMISSION TO BH

1. Confirmed diagnosis of AIDS.
2. Exhausted all personal resources in search for quality housing in a supportive atmosphere.
3. Unable to locate quality housing due to limited financial resources.
4. Physical health permits applicant to perform activities of daily living. Applicant must be able to feed, bathe and care for self.
5. Under the care of a primary physician for the treatment of AIDS.
6. Shows motivation in aggressively combating the illness.
7. Has the capacity to function in a group residential facility.
8. Understands the concept of community living and agrees to participate in this milieu.
9. Agrees to contribute, as much as physically possible, toward the maintenance and smooth operation of the facility.
10. Does not have the benefit of a personal support network to assist in the day to day coping with the illness.
11. Agrees to pay 45% of total income to BH for room and meals. The aforementioned percentage of income utilized for rent is subject to change at the beginning of each year.
12. Has read, understands and agrees to follow the policies stipulated in the Bonaventure House Policy Manual for residents.
13. Has made application for public benefits (social security or public assistance) when financial resources are limited.
14. Has submitted a completed BH application with all supporting documentation.

Bonaventure House recognizes the fact that not all applicants who apply for admission will be suitable for our environment. Therefore, it is our responsibility to deny admission to individuals whom, based upon our assessment, we believe would not succeed in the type of environment which we have to offer. These individuals include but are not limited to:

SPECIFIC DENIAL GUIDELINES FOR ADMISSION TO BH

1. Applicants who do not meet all the above listed criteria in the guidelines for admission to BH.
2. Applicants who for any reason would require a more structured, supervised setting than BH could provide.
3. Applicants who are actively abusing alcohol or substances and refuse to follow a recovery program or treatment plan.
4. Recovering substance abusers who refuse to follow a recovery program or treatment plan.
5. Applicants who have a prior history of mental illness which indicates their inability to function independently in an unsupervised group residential setting.
6. Applicants who have a history of behavior which has endangered others and may pose a threat to the general safety of BH and its residents.
7. Applicants experiencing dementia associated with HIV infection which would require these individuals to have closer supervision than BH could provide.
8. Applicants who refuse to maintain a relationship with a primary physician.

FIG. 2.1.   Bonaventure House Admissions Statement.

bed, he never lost his spirit. I had always envisioned being alone and dying, but BH cured that. I know I will never have to be alone when that time comes.

In numerous discussions with residents and staff, the primary fear associated with having AIDS was dying alone. Even for those abandoned by family, socially isolated, and left homeless, the fear of dying alone represented the ultimate desertion. BH thus offers residents a sense of hope, which, although associated primarily with surviving until a cure is found or living longer than expected, is also evoked in reference to the quality of life—talk about dying with dignity and in the comfort of others. As Timothy McCormick, Chief Executive Officer of Alexian Brothers Bonaventure House/Center for Assisted Living, pointed out, "Someone will be there to hold your hand, someone will be there no matter what. That's a hell of a thing to offer someone who comes in here. No matter what else happens . . . you won't be alone when you die."

Negative expectations about living at BH reflect two major concerns. First, people are concerned about entering a place where they will be "around a lot of dead and dying people." As Edward noted in the previous portrait, when he was living alone he didn't have to "think that much about AIDS." Many residents expressed fear that BH would be "just a bunch of real sick people" and a hospice "where you wait to die."

People are also concerned about the loss of autonomy, foreseeing BH as a place that runs their lives. Clyde said, "I thought it was an institution . . . [that was] going to orientate and run my life every hour of the day." When asked what he gave up to move to BH, Barry, a rather self-sufficient newcomer, noted, "A certain amount of freedom, a certain amount of self-determination. Not being able to choose when you're hungry, when you want to eat"—or, for that matter, what you want to eat (see Fig. 2.2). Although there are some food options, the diversity in food preferences, eating habits, and dietary restrictions leads to some dissatisfaction. For example, Mexican and soul food are rarely served, and highly spicy or fatty foods are limited, due to digestive problems for PWAs. This issue, along with many others, such as loss of privacy, was, in Pete's words, an inevitable result of living "with 25 roommates at one time."

Loss of autonomy and a better life are felt most deeply by the more affluent residents and those attached psychologically and/or emotionally to their own apartments or houses. Prior research indicates the powerful symbolic force of material possessions in constructing the self (Belk, 1988), because possessions provide people with a sense of identity and control over their lives. Although dispossession can be a letting go of one's former self, as in the case of divorce (see McAlexander, 1991; McAlexander, Schouten, & Roberts, 1993), it also can be a ritual of bereavement for the social role one has lost. When asked what he left behind in order to move to BH, Branden noted bitterly:

A total lifestyle from the word "go." My home was sold. I had to pack up all my possessions and put them in storage. I have a black and white TV. In storage, I have three color TVs with remote. I left everything behind. Of course, Steve and I were together for 13 years. That's the biggest blow—I lost my lover [who died

FIG. 2.2. Although some food options are provided (such as two main courses), meals at Bonaventure House are a communal affair, served in buffet style at set times of the day (photograph by Paul Merideth).

of AIDS], my home, and my lifestyle. Affluence is a legitimate loss, as I've learned. It's grievable.

Branden clung to his desire to move out, keeping most of his possessions in storage throughout his stay at BH, and keeping his room in sparse disarray until his death. He kept one long, very expensive mink coat that he wore with panache throughout the winter, almost as though it were a symbol of his defiance in the face of social and material loss. As Branden mentioned on another occasion, "A couple of people make smart-ass remarks about that stupid coat. . . . I've lived better, and it's gone now. What do they want me to do, give that coat away?"

Whether it be a fur coat, a book collection, or a beat-up car, loss can be painful, despite the market value of the goods. Material loss can also represent one more restriction in daily life activities at BH. Tyler, a resident whose major loss was his pots and pans and love for cooking, recounted his passion: "I'm one of those fanatics who goes out and buys a couscoussiere because I wanted to cook a Moroccan dinner one night. Even if I had the couscoussiere here, who would know how to make it, except me? Who would eat it, except me?"

Regardless of the hopes and/or fears that accompany their initial entry, moving into BH poses innumerable adjustments for newcomers in expectations, coping with everyday life, and even personal identity. As the next section shows, feelings about moving into BH also entail the gnarled entanglement of dependence and independence.

BURDENING OTHERS: SEEKING NEW CAREGIVERS

Although the notion of *loss* (e.g., of autonomy and privacy, material possessions, and social support) is a major theme in the anticipatory phase of entering BH, there is also the persistent concern, in Randy's words, of "no longer being a burden to one's family and friends." Granted, many residents have been abandoned by loved ones, but in the majority of our interviews, we found a deep concern for not becoming dependent on, and burdensome to, others. Fear of dependency is thus a strong motivation for entering BH.

All close relationships, regardless of their level of intimacy, are governed and sustained by a norm of reciprocity. However, the capacity to reciprocate can shift dramatically when coping with an illness. As Fruend and McGuire (1995) explained:

> Much of our web of social relationships is predicated on the assumption that members will be able to reciprocate, that one member will not be utterly dependent upon others, and that all give and receive. Some illnesses undermine the assumption of reciprocity and thus make social relationships precarious. Losing independence is threatening to one's sense of self not just because of pride in self-sufficiency (a related value in our culture), but more because it

impairs one's ability to participate as an equal in important social relationships. Valued friendships and social roles become strained or lost altogether. (pp. 145–146)

This norm of reciprocity is particularly important in the exchange of social support (Greenberg & Shapiro, 1971). When people are not in a position to reciprocate assistance, they can experience feelings of indebtedness and even powerlessness. Barry, for example, was deeply concerned with meeting his responsibilities in the apartment he shared with his sister prior to entering BH: "I was looking at a way to relieve her of feeling obligated, to not go on with what *she* needs to do for herself because of me. I don't want to be a burden to anybody. That had a lot to do with what prompted me to apply."

Randy, who came from a devoted family and had numerous friends who offered housing, was concerned not only about the stress that his illness would cause, but dreaded being homebound and socially isolated during the day. Due to acute infection of the gastrointestinal track, Randy became very lethargic and started to lose weight. His sister "found it very difficult to accept the fact that I looked healthy, but I had absolutely no energy," which resulted in mutual frustration.

Having watched others die from AIDS is not an uncommon experience for many of the residents, and this has a profound effect on their desire not to be a burden. Mac witnessed his wife, daughter, and countless friends contract the disease and die within a month or two of each other, and decided to withdraw from his family's support:

My family was accessible. I abandoned them because I felt guilty because I had AIDS. I felt dirty. Moral support and spiritual support, just being there for me was what they could have offered. They couldn't have offered me much in terms of housing or money, but they would have been there for me. But I chose to stay away from them because I felt guilty. I felt dirty and I felt dead. Why do I want to put my family through this dying process? I had just witnessed it with my wife. I had lived through it and it was ugly.

Mac was a resident for about 7 months, but he returned to using drugs and alcohol, and was asked to leave BH. As we review his thoughts, we are struck by how deeply affected he was by the pain and suffering he had seen, and by his own anxiety about death:

I don't really worry about dying because we have to die. I worry about dying in pain. I don't want to lay in bed, getting emaciated, having people take care of you, morphine drips, and people sad and feeling sorry. I don't want all that. If I could choose, I would like to walk out this door and get hit by a truck. If you're gonna tell me, "Mac, you're gonna die on March 15, 1992," fine. Just don't make me sit between now and then. It's the part of the disease that really pisses me off. It's one part I don't understand about life in general, why do we have to suffer?

Because AIDS takes a toll on family and social networks, most residents are already familiar with the burden of suffering. Anxiety about pain runs deep, as do mixed emotions of comfort and guilt in having family and friends nearby. One of the most profound paradoxes in coping with illness in close relationships is the knowledge that even though one may be cared for, distress is unavoidable.

HANDLING DIVERSITY:
THE LITMUS TEST OF COMMUNITY LIFE

In all our years at BH, the most striking feature of the house is the incredible diversity of people, many of whom, given a choice, would never associate with one another, let alone choose to live together. Walking into the communal dining room where residents tend to congregate, the diversity in race, ethnicity, and gender is apparent (see Fig. 2.3). Speech patterns reveal the ethnic diversity, where Puerto Rican Spanish, Polish, and Black English blend at a single table. Sexual orientation, which may be blatant or unspoken, is but one indicator of sexual diversity. Expressed longing for long-term intimacy or professed state

FIG. 2.3.   Walking into the communal dining room during dinner reveals the diverse group of people who live and work at Bonaventure House. Table conversations range from politics to work-related issues to sexual innuendoes and jokes. Although people are free to sit where they like, as with any communal setting, cliques do form. For example, residents who smoke congregate together at designated tables
(photograph by Paul Merideth).

of celibacy; declared preference for conventional and unconventional sexual practices (e.g., cross-dressing, S & M); and jokes, crass remarks, or boasting of sexual exploits are but a few variations that reveal the range of sexualities, regardless of preference for heterosexual or homosexual partner, or both. Table conversations about corporate work, high school teaching, monastic life, waitressing, prostitution, and unemployment reveal an array of socioeconomic backgrounds. Whereas some residents talk about upcoming trips abroad, others have difficulty paying bus fare to go downtown.

The health status of incoming and veteran residents also varies considerably, adding another layer to the diversity felt in the house. Although BH is designed as a residence for assisted living (accepting only those who are still ambulatory and physically independent, some of whom remain healthy and active for years), new residents have died within a few days of entry. Due to the uncertain nature of opportunistic infections, residents may arrive in relatively good health and then deteriorate suddenly.

When there is a waiting list to get in to BH, the staff can be more selective about whom to admit; but when there are open beds and no waiting list, people who are very sick are offered a room. This short-term entry and loss can generate a lot of resentment, for it can make BH feel more like a hospice than a home. Because a hospice is viewed by residents as a place to die, this distinction is critical and has important ramifications both for newcomers' entry and integration into residential life, and for veterans' views of BH and their reactions to newcomers. The house also provides a different experience depending on the health status of veteran residents. When many residents are extremely sick, a heaviness prevails, a feeling that is almost negligible when residents are generally healthy. There is, however, as we see later, no predictable pattern to the ebb and flow of health in this house.

Profound variations in social networks and support systems cut across the heterogeneity of health status and the demographics of race, ethnicity, gender, and sexuality. Residents may have intact or estranged intimate relationships with parents, brothers and sisters, spouses, lovers, and children. They might have extended, loving family and friendship networks, or they might be social isolates.

Only a minority of the residents we surveyed (22.0%) were involved in a romantic relationship, often because they had lost their significant others to AIDS. In the course of our volunteer work, two residents shared their scrapbooks. Each had been in a long-term relationship for over 10 years, and both had lost not only their lovers, but also most of their friends. Mara remembers the afternoon when Branden shared his scrapbook with her. When he got to a picture of his friends smiling on the deck of a gorgeous yacht, he began pointing out all those who had died from AIDS. Branden spoke often of his long-term partner for whom he continued to grieve:

Yes, I am incredibly lonely. I just had no idea what it was going to be like to be without him. None. I still can't comprehend it. I'm so tired of people telling me

I'm going to get over it. He's been dead a year and 2 months. How am I going to get over someone who was half my life for half my life?

Social loss also occurs due to abandonment by family and friends. The poignancy of such loss is captured by those residents who continue to keep portraits on their nightstands of the families that abandoned them, or who wait longingly for relatives and friends that never visit, even as death approaches.

The threat of abandonment is so powerful that some residents disguise the purpose of BH from family and friends. Inadvertently, for those who have remained silent about their sexual orientation, drug usage, and/or HIV or AIDS status, becoming a resident at BH can be an "outing" process. In this case, the secret is revealed not by others, as in the typical outing process, but by residence. Some residents thus choose not to reveal much to friends and family about BH. Scott, profiled at the beginning of this chapter, spoke of a history of rejection, and his deep concern over a similar reaction if his children were to know he had AIDS and lived in a residential facility for PWAs:

I have three [kids]. I normally see them every week and talk to them daily on the phone. None of my kids know about the virus. I've been really dishonest to them about that. I told them it was like a facility for people who have cancer or some chronic illness. I would prefer breaking the news to them before they have to hear it on TV and see, "Oh, my Dad has AIDS." I have this fear if I told them, then they would reject me. When I was growing up, my father accused my mother of cheating on him, so he kind of disowned me. . . . When I became infected in '86, when you would go to the hospital, they [the staff] wouldn't even come into your room. My mother was deceased, my father was deceased, my wife was deceased. I had a lot of fear of losing them [his kids] if I revealed it to them, so I chose not to do so.

Even giving out the phone number of the house becomes an act of self-disclosure. Pete, who chose not to disclose his illness to others, was waiting for his personal phone and refused to give out the house number, "'cause as soon as you hear 'Bonaventure House,' you think, 'Oh, a place for AIDS,' and from there people don't want to associate with you, and you lose what you did have." Needless to say, he did not invite friends to the house in order to keep his HIV status a secret.

Finally, there is wide variation in the extent to which residents socialize outside of BH. Some maintain active social lives, but there is a sizeable population (27.1% of those surveyed) that socializes very little or not at all outside the house. Obviously, one reason is their illness, but there are also those who define themselves as "homebodies" or who are constrained by a lack of disposable income (39.6% of residents surveyed indicated they did not have enough money to go out and do things). In some cases, residents may be self-conscious about their disfigurement and the treatment they receive in public places. This response is consistent with what others have reported: "Some people with disabilities report that because of treatment in public places, they have, for instance, taken such measures as going outside only when accompanied, avoiding any but the most necessary of purchases" (Gardner, 1991, p. 259).

Although the benefits of diversity are many, it can make communication more difficult and increase interpersonal problems (see Kirchmeyer, 1993; Kirchmeyer & Cohen, 1992; Ruhe & Eatman, 1977; Vaid-Raizada, 1985). People often assume that having AIDS is the great equalizer, the tie that binds the members of BH together, but they forget about the enormous differences in background, health status, existing social support networks, and expectations about living at BH that make interpersonal connection and community building extremely difficult. Several of the anticipatory images noted previously reveal the despair and fear of moving in to a place in which numerous residents note that the only common bond is the virus, or even less. As Robbin shared, "I just don't feel there's any mutual ground other than 'What's for dinner?'" Branden, an educated, outspoken, gay professional, saw his expectation of BH as a "Boys' Town" shattered soon after his arrival:

> I was talking to P. [another resident] once, and she said, "Honey, you have no idea what it's like to peddle Black pussy on the street when it's 40 below." Should I take her to see Tosca or the symphony next week? I really don't feel like I have anything in common with the majority of the people that are here now.

Managing diversity is perhaps the most important challenge facing contemporary organizations and other collectives (see Allen, 1995; Boyer & Webb, 1992; Coleman, 1990; Cox & Blake, 1991; Fernandez, 1991; Frey & Barge, 1997; Jackson & Associates, 1992; Lewan, 1990). This observation is especially true for organizations like BH that strive to promote community, where "interpersonal relations are characterized by common understanding of the meaningfulness of differences" (Rothenbuhler, 1991, p. 64), and, in a democratic manner, respect the multiple voices of its members. "The litmus test for a democratic organization," Eisenberg (1994) claimed, "is its ability to handle diversity" (p. 281).

The difficulty of managing diversity at BH cannot be underestimated. Perhaps establishing community under these circumstances is unrealistic, or a pipe dream, as Ann, a much-beloved staff member, explained:

> We're asking people to do something [become socially cohesive] that they really can't do. These are people who are chronically ill with many mood changes, not only because of HIV, but drug-induced because of their medications, and electrolyte imbalance-induced, character disorders that were never diagnosed. We have people who lived on the street . . . we have a person who never went to high school, can't write, can't read, can only sign his name, up to a PhD, and then all the layers in the middle. We ask all these people to live together. I mean, general society people can't live together like that.

The problems associated with diversity at BH have the potential to rip apart this community. Indeed, at Bailey House, a residence for PWAs in New York City, the problems between gay men and intravenous drug users became so great that one resident suggested that these two groups be segregated by floor (C. Brown, 1992). Neither Bailey House nor Bonaventure House, however, has resorted to such tactics. In the case of BH, staff and residents have found ways to facilitate the entry experience, practices that offer safety nets and create collective views that help socialize new residents into community life.

AVOIDING DROP-SHIPPING: PARACHUTES FOR ENTRY

Newcomers to any organization invariably experience some reality shock (Hughes, 1958) or surprise (Louis, 1980), a truism for new residents at BH. Louis noted that during the entry period of organizational life, "there is no gradual exposure and no way to confront the situation a little at a time. Rather, the newcomer's senses are simultaneously inundated with many unfamiliar cues" (p. 230). This "'encounter' with the unfamiliar or ambiguous" (Teboul, 1994, p. 193), which goes by many names—ambiguity (Norton, 1975), equivocality (Weick, 1979), error or disconfirmation (Argyris & Schon, 1978), gap (Dervin, 1983), and situational anxiety (Argyle, Furnham, & Graham, 1981)—can be a stressful period.

Before BH developed formal orientation procedures, learning the ropes occurred through informal conversations with residents, staff, and volunteers. Although this approach was sufficient for some, many newcomers remained bewildered by the cognitive and social demands of this highly structured, interdependent, collective-living situation. Clyde, a resident, spoke critically of this laissez-faire approach to socialization:

> Sometimes I think when they bring new people in here it's like they're drop-shipping. They're putting a parachute on their back and pushing them out of the airplane and saying, "There's your survival kit, survive." That doesn't work with a lot of people. It just doesn't. What happens is that the damage caused by those first few days can take up to a month [to repair].

In response to entry problems, staff and residents began developing more formal practices for selecting and assimilating newcomers into the house. Because residents enter individually as vacancies arise, and their terms of stay vary, the practices are individual rather than collective. It is difficult, therefore, to standardize this experience or speak of a cohort effect (the impact of a group of people who enter at the same time). However, a number of practices are commonly employed.

Prior to entering BH, a person fills out an application form that asks about such things as personal background and health history. The applicant then receives an information packet about the house. He or she is interviewed by the staff, who look especially for people oriented toward community living. If the person meets the requirements, he or she is invited to tour the house, meet residents, and share a meal. Hopefully, these audition practices (Sigman, 1985–1986) facilitate a self-selection process and help newcomers establish realistic, rather than inflated, expectations.

Contact with residents prior to entry is a delicate issue. In the case where a room is unavailable, an applicant is put on a waiting list. In reality, he or she is waiting for someone to die. If visits to BH occur prematurely, the person may inadvertently meet the resident whom he or she will replace. Such delays and encounters add another layer of stress to the applicant's suspended fate.

Newcomers' entry is an unspoken, sensitive area for veteran residents—a reminder of loss. Timothy J. Budz, Executive Director of BH, pointed to the dilemma and consideration given to applicants' visits:

> They [prospective newcomers] have been coming for meals. We're trying to integrate them into this facility. Earlier, we talked about them even attending house meetings to see what kind of issues there are. It was the residents who brought up that attending house meetings would not be good because the newcomer would be sitting with his or her peers, and would know that one of them would be dying and he or she would be replacing that exact person. So the residents suggested it would be okay for newcomers to come to lunch or dinner once in awhile, but they didn't want them fully integrated into the house prior to that. The residents are pretty much in tune to these things and understand what's happening.

Once situated in the house, newcomers quickly experience or witness the everyday physical and emotional support residents offer one another (see Fig. 2.4), practices discussed further in the next chapter. Efforts to formalize supportive relationships in a buddy system that pairs each newcomer with an experienced veteran, however, have met with mixed success. Because the buddy system is strictly voluntary, only a few, capable veteran residents show interest in participating. Newcomers also vary in their desire to receive formal assistance from others. For those whose identity is grounded in rugged individualism, being assigned a buddy may evoke feelings of dependence. For the 53% of the residents surveyed who speak favorably about the buddy system, its major contributions are: reducing newcomers' anxiety about learning the explicit rules and regulations, teaching them about implicit rules (e.g., "who to go to for what"), and helping them to integrate into a social clique.

As mentioned in the last chapter, newcomers must attend a weekly support group for the first 6 weeks of residency, and those who previously abused drugs and alcohol must attend weekly recovery groups throughout their stay. Many residents find their social niche in these support groups, and continue to participate long after the 6 weeks end; in some cases, these groups become their new family.

FIG. 2.4.   One invariably is struck by the physical and emotional support that members of Bonaventure House offer one another, even in public spaces, such as the dining room. At night, when staff, volunteers, and visitors are gone, the house takes on more of a cozy atmosphere (photograph by Paul Merideth).

A PLACE TO LIVE WITH AIDS:
THE SYMBOLIC CONSTRUCTION OF COMMUNITY

All organizations are faced with the problem of developing a collective image or identity, "a shared understanding of what the organization is about and how it should operate" (Berg, 1985, p. 296). Frake (1977) called this process *map making and navigation*, as it helps new and veteran members chart a course and coordinate actions (see S. Albert & Whetten, 1985; Cheney, 1991, 1992; Cheney & Tompkins, 1987; Cheney & Vibbert, 1987; Deetz, 1992; Tompkins & Cheney, 1985). As Treadwell and Harrison (1994) maintained, "While any specific individual's image of an organization is ultimately idiosyncratic, members must share some knowledge of the organization's goals or mission and ways of achieving them if coordination and a common sense of direction [are] to be achieved" (p. 65).

Because the mission of BH envisioned by the Alexian Brothers is to foster community life that promotes a holistic approach to health (e.g., physical, emotional, and spiritual), its collective image goes beyond the mere functional notion of a residential facility. The construction of this shared identity occurs via *symbolic management*, the creation, interpretation, negotiation, and communication of meaning (see Pfeiffer, 1981; Sackmann, 1990), as displayed in significant symbols, stories, metaphors, rituals, and fantasies, among other forms (see Eisenberg & Goodall, 1994). Barnlund (1988) noted that "every culture attempts to create a 'universe of discourse' for its members, a way in which people can interpret their experience and convey it to one another" (p. 11). Organizational symbolism thus reflects "those aspects of an organization that its members use to reveal or make comprehensible the unconscious feelings, images, and values that are inherent in the organization" (Dandridge, Mitroff, & Joyce, 1980, p. 77). Here, we focus on three forms of strategic symbolic management at BH: the construction of a rhetorical vision of BH as a place to live with AIDS; the acceptance of the significant symbol of community; and the retelling of success stories that become part of the house legacy.

The rhetorical vision of the house is evoked frequently in everyday discourse in the phrase "a place to live with AIDS." Terrance recounted his first day, sitting alone in his new room, wondering if he had made a good choice. Maria, another resident, knocked on the door, poked her head in, and said, "Well, I hope you came here to live and not to die," a reassurance that made him realize that things would be OK. This vision is more than a rhetorical veil; it not only emphasizes the importance of remaining active and healthy, it also wards off the shroud of inevitable and imminent mortality.

The notion of living with AIDS is especially critical given the wide variation in residents' psychosocial adjustment to having AIDS, particularly in terms of their knowledge, acceptance, and willingness to engage in a prohealthy lifestyle. To begin, knowledge about AIDS among BH residents ranges from minimal (e.g., Jason said he "knows only what he has heard on television") to borderline expert (Randy had a clinical background in medicine), often underscored by level of education and acceptance of the illness. Charlotte, a grandmother who had been a resident for 5 months at the time of our interview, recounted how BH helped her understand her illness:

> I thought it [BH] was going to be hell, like a nursing home. They have helped me with my disease. Instead of sadness and sorrow, they've brought happiness . . . and I still have life left in me. . . . I had a nephew die of AIDS, he was 21. I saw him die so fast, and my husband died so fast, I thought it was going to do me the same. I was ignorant on these things.

Clearly, if one's understanding of AIDS is framed only as a death sentence, then it is unlikely that such knowledge is an asset in coping with the illness. Charlotte's comment reveals how living at BH enabled her to reframe the illness from a focus on dying to one of living with AIDS. This reframing is more than simply calling a cup half full or half empty—it is a profound shift of negative psychic energy to more positive and healing attitudes about life.

Although knowledge about the illness is addressed by educational seminars offered at BH, acceptance is much more complex and can affect how incoming residents view and adjust to community life. According to the Executive Director, incoming residents frequently arrive very angry about the loss of control and autonomy in their lives due to the illness.

As volunteers, we received training to sensitize us to some of the losses and emotional reactions residents experience during the typical course of the disease. Bill, a veteran volunteer, described one of the powerful exercises used during the training sessions:

> One of the exercises we completed during training was to write down the 10 most important things to us. It could be anything material, spiritual, or even feelings we cherished. Once the list was completed, the facilitator led us through the AIDS disease process, and, at various steps of the process, we had to cross off our list the things we had previously indicated as being the 10 most important things in our lives. When we were finally told that we were not in such great shape and had several serious health problems, we only had one or two items remaining on our list. At that point, the facilitator said, "Welcome to Bonaventure House." I think of that exercise often.

Living with AIDS not only entails psychosocial adjustments to losses experienced, but the commitment to take care of one's health. Caring for one's health is not merely a personal issue; it has collective consequences. Several residents voiced fears about contagious diseases and harmful bacteria that placed them at risk. Scott noted:

> There's a lot of things that you can catch that are in this house. If a person ain't hygienic and don't wash his hands after he goes to the toilet, and stuff like that, it could be on the serving spoon in the dinner line and then I could get it, and I don't need none of that stuff. . . . Hygiene is real important.

Fear is also expressed by staff members. Tim Budz shared his personal dilemma about working at the house: "I've begun to think, when we've had a couple of [TB] cases identified, what does that mean for my health? What does that mean for my family's health? What types of risks am I taking by being present in this building?"

Concerns over health care go beyond complaints, fears, and warnings, for the ideology of living with AIDS requires specific behaviors on the part of BH community members. For example, staff and volunteers are tested for TB every 6 months, special containers are provided in residents' rooms for the disposal of needles and blood products, and signs are posted in the bathrooms to wash hands and clean the toilets and showers after use. Residents are told by staff to cover open sores and rashes, and to wear masks if they are coughing due to a cold, flu, or infection. Gloves are readily available for emergencies. During an incident in the kitchen, a resident cut his finger while preparing food and began to bleed profusely. He quickly washed, bandaged, and gloved his hand, disposed of the contaminated food, and cleaned the table. Occasionally, concern over hygiene focuses on more personal behaviors, particularly with residents who are incontinent or who do not bathe regularly. In short, attention to hygienic practices borders on the vigilant, and taking care of oneself is a lesson taught quickly to violators.

A second form of strategic symbolic management by which organizations, including BH, create a shared identity for newcomers is offering significant symbols, especially new metaphors, for understanding the organizational culture and the newcomer's role in it (see Donnellon, Gray, & Bongon, 1986; Koch & Deetz, 1981; Riley, 1983, 1985; Sackmann, 1989; Trujillo, 1985; Vaughn, 1995). A metaphor, in this context, is a figure of speech in which a word or phrase that denotes one object is applied to another. Lakoff and Johnson (1980) argued that metaphors define and create new realities. This result is particularly evident in constructing new identities among organizational members:

> [Metaphors] convene new meanings by fitting them into imagination-stimulation messages. Their role consists partly in reducing the uncertainty produced by an encounter with what is new; they refer to something that is better known than the object of the metaphor. They can be seen as shortcuts in explanation as they are used to evoke a single image that encompasses the entire range of meanings of the object. . . . It is the metaphor's evocative, and not reflective, power that is most important (Geertz, 1973). Metaphors are the material of which future identities are made. (Czarniawska-Jorges, 1994, pp. 206–207)

Organizational metaphors delineate "the interpretive frameworks of organizational members" (Conrad, 1983, p. 187) and, moreover, help develop a unique group identification that bonds members (Larwood, 1992). Metaphors accomplish this by establishing new territories and identities: "Once boundaries have been drawn, the possibility of relationship emerges. Without boundaries, there can be no relationship" (Smith & Berg, 1987, p. 103). When successful, metaphors communicate organizational philosophy, values, and beliefs (Cheney & Vibbert, 1987; Morgan, 1986; Siehl, 1985), help develop a common organizational identity (Cheney, 1983), and promote organizational commitment (Mowday, Steers, & Porter, 1979; Sass & Canary, 1991).

When BH was founded, the metaphor of *family* was used widely by staff and residents to describe the interpersonal relations between house members. However, this metaphor triggered many negative reactions among residents. Branden screamed, "Family, schmamily. I hate that concept. We're not family. We're a bunch of dying homosexuals, for the most part, with a multitude of personality problems." For those from dysfunctional families, the term carried negative connotations; others preferred to reserve it only for their kin; and several residents thought the term sugar-coated the vast differences that separate people in the house. Even Ron, one of the staff members, humorously commented, "If we are a family, it's a cross between the Addams family and the Manson family."

Neither staff nor residents perceive themselves as being in a parent–child relationship, as in a typical family structure. When asked on the questionnaires to indicate their level of agreement (on a 5-point scale) with terms, articulated in interviews, that might describe their relationship, *parents* was the lowest rated term for residents and the second lowest rated term for staff; *family* was not rated much higher (see Table 2.1). According to Budz, staff members believe

TABLE 2.1.
Perceptions of Relationships Between Staff and Residents

	RESIDENTS' VIEWS OF RELATIONSHIPS WITH STAFF (n = 59) *Question: On the whole, when you think of staff, do you see them as:*						STAFF'S VIEWS OF RELATIONSHIPS WITH RESIDENTS (n = 27) *Question: On the whole, when you think of the residents, do you see yourself as:*				
	Strongly Disagree/ Disagree	Strongly Agree/ Agree	SD	Mean	Rank		Rank	Mean	SD	Strongly Agree/ Agree	Strongly Disagree/ Disagree
Professionals	5.1%	84.7%	0.74	4.05	1		1	4.26	.76	88.9%	3.7%
Community Members	18.7%	62.7%	1.07	3.61	2		2	3.85	.72	81.5%	7.4%
Caregivers	13.6%	61.1%	1.03	3.61	2		3	3.63	1.15	66.7%	22.2%
Friends	20.3%	59.4%	1.05	3.50	4		4	33.3	1.07	55.6%	22.2%
Bosses/Supervisors	45.8%	40.7%	1.22	2.87	5		6	2.33	1.18	29.6%	63.0%
Family	49.7%	39.0%	1.33	2.83	6		5	2.65	1.23	38.5%	50.0%
Police	64.4%	18.7%	1.11	2.38	7		8	1.74	1.06	14.8%	85.2%
Parents	75.5%	17.0%	1.10	2.22	8		7	2.26	1.35	22.2%	66.7%

they need to be "experts in reparenting, giving residents a new experience of nurturing, of love, of limit setting, and of structure. Reparenting, however, doesn't mean being a parent in the sense of treating residents as children."

Once the house shifted from a small, highly homogeneous group to a larger, more diversified population, around 1992, the family metaphor was offically dropped. Robert Rybicki, the Executive Director at that time, noted the shift: "It doesn't seem like a family. It's not a gay, all White, male club anymore."

Although long-term residents, staff, and volunteers still reminisce about the camaraderie of the "good ole days," shared demographics and lifestyles were certainly not givens for creating a family-like atmosphere. Volatile personalities and subgroup differences (e.g., the cross-dressers, the more closeted gays, the leather queens, etc.) were often sources of conflict and clique formation. Even within highly homogeneous groups, individuals often differ in their beliefs, attitudes, values, and behaviors, and subgroups sometimes form around those differences. However, group harmony is even more difficult to attain in the face of significant demographic diversity, where common goals and ways to achieve them do not necessarily exist in the beginning but, instead, must be created.

In place of the family metaphor, a conscious effort is made by staff and residents to use the significant symbol of *community*. For example, promotional materials about BH reference it as a community, and the term is part of the everyday discourse of the house. Community acknowledges a very different connection among BH members from that of family. No longer trapped in the terminology of kin, community reflects the diversity of BH and the many roles that residents and staff assume. Clyde, a resident, invoked a metaphor to explain community: "Community is like a forest. You've got to have a little bit of everything or the forest dies." Alternatively, Pete saw BH as "a jungle, a zoo sometimes." Although there is a shared identity of BH as a community, its nature is evaluated quite differently by various members.

The significant symbol of community generates some limited negative reactions on the part of residents. Scott, for example, was "tired of having community shoved down our throats." Overwhelmingly, however, this symbol is well accepted by the members of this residence. Indeed, when asked to evaluate 10 symbols that described BH, all of which emerged from interviews with staff and residents, *community* was rated the highest (see Table 2.2). Residents and staff also see the staff as professionals, community members, and caregivers (see Table 2.1). As can be seen, there was almost perfect agreement on the rankings of these concepts by residents and staff about what BH and the staff's roles are and are not.

The rhetorical vision of BH as a place to live with AIDS, and the significant symbol of community are sustained in many ways by the third form of symbolic strategic management—the stories that staff and residents tell about previous residents who lived there. MacIntyre (1981) claimed that we are "essentially a story-telling animal" (p. 201); as *homo narrans*, we organize experience into stories with plots, central characters, and action sequences that carry implicit or explicit lessons (see W. R. Fisher, 1984, 1987).

TABLE 2.2.
Metaphors Used to Describe Bonaventure House

BONAVENTURE HOUSE IS LIKE A:

	RESIDENTS (n = 59)						STAFF (n = 27)			
	Strongly Disagree/Disagree	Strongly Agree/Agree	SD	Mean	Rank		Rank	Mean	SD	Strongly Agree/Agree	Strongly Disagree/Disagree
Community	15.3%	72.9%	1.02	3.68	1	1	3.82	.62	77.8%	3.7%
Home	18.7%	69.5%	1.16	3.67	2	2	3.59	1.03	70.4%	25.9%
Family	20.4%	62.8%	1.13	3.53	3	4	3.37	.79	48.1%	14.8%
Institution	44.1%	11.9%	1.22	2.86	4	3	3.41	.93	63.0%	22.2%
Dormitory	47.4%	33.9%	1.26	2.67	5	5	2.26	1.10	17.5%	63.0%
Shelter	62.7%	18.6%	1.10	2.28	6	7	2.08	.85	7.7%	76.9%
Hospice	62.7%	15.3%	1.05	2.26	7	5	2.26	.86	11.1%	70.3%
Hotel	78.0%	10.2%	.91	1.96	8	8	1.63	.79	3.7%	88.9%
Hospital	88.1%	1.7%	.62	1.75	9	9	1.33	.48	-	100%
Prison	86.5%	-	.61	1.67	10	10	1.22	.42	-	100%

Stories about previous residents that carry implicit values abound at BH. One favorite story is about Mannie, a gruff streetperson with a 25-year history of injecting drugs, who refused to accept his illness and, on the first day of his arrival at BH, alienated just about everyone with his loud, racist remarks and the Confederate flag sewn to his hat. Eventually, with support from residents and staff, he turned around and became a very giving and beloved house member who took care of himself and other residents, serving as a role model. He was, according to the Executive Director, "one of the most profound individuals we ever did see come through our doors." His legend lives on long after his death.

When told in a group setting, a story like the one about Mannie is a "creative and imaginative shared interpretation of events that fulfills a group psychological need" (Bormann, 1986, p. 221). Stories help group members achieve *symbolic convergence*, the sharing of a common social reality (see Bormann, 1983, 1986, 1996), by communicating organizational norms and values (Trujillo, 1985) and coordinating the activities of members toward common goals (J. Martin, 1982; Wilkens, 1984). Stories are particularly effective for assimilating new members into an organization's culture (M. H. Brown, 1985; Stohl, 1986): "One step short of 'learning by doing,' new employees [newcomers] learn by hearing about *others* doing" (Meyer, 1995, p. 211).

Stories, moreover, are multivocalic in that they are often told by different groups for very different purposes. For example, we complimented Tyler on his stuffed, but organized room, and he laughed, saying that he has been told it looks like Mannie's old room. He never met Mannie, but felt he knew him because of all he heard about him. But Tyler also resented how the staff members constantly spoke of Mannie's transformation as *their* success story. He said adamantly, "Hell, they didn't do it, it was the circumstances."

During our conversations with residents it was not uncommon to hear references to residents who had passed away, and occasionally to incidents that became, not just part of the BH folklore, but also *illness tales*—the collective interpretations that ease the stigma of deviant behavior and unusual symptoms due to AIDS by conversion to the absurd. For example, Sean, an already rather eccentric resident, became mentally disoriented toward the latter stages of his illness. In telling the story, a resident who had never met him laughed about how Sean was found "butt naked" in the foyer.

Success stories and illness tales told over and over again become part of the BH legacy. For both newcomers and veterans, these stories help create and sustain a unified rhetorical vision of BH as a community where people live, not die, with AIDS.

LOW-KEY OR GUNG-HO: COPING WITH COMMUNITY LIFE

Adjustment to the shared identity of community life, and the rhetoric of BH as a place to live with AIDS, varies according to the individual resident. Prior work on organizational socialization points to the various roles that newcomers assume, from simply taking on prior roles (e.g., "custodians") to becoming innovators who try to change the organization (Louis, 1980). Coping strategies thus range on a continuum from passive to active (see Ashford, 1986; Ashford & Cummings, 1985; Comer, 1991; Morrison, 1993, 1995; Ostroff & Kozlowski, 1992).

Although newcomers at BH engage in a number of active strategies, such as information-seeking (Jablin, 1987; V. Miller & Jablin, 1991; Morrison, 1995), they run the risk of social rejection if these strategies are used too much. We sometimes heard veterans voice suspicion of newcomers who "try too hard" by being too friendly too soon. The most prominent way of easing into community life is keeping a low profile, which often includes a mixture of withdrawal and observing and monitoring other residents. On arrival, Pete was advised to "just sit back and watch and listen, and you will learn the ins and outs of the house. That's basically it." Jeremiah described his initiation through hibernation: "When I first got here, it took a little bit of adjusting, and I would go through these phases where I just hibernated completely. Now I've kinda adjusted and balanced it out right to where I will peek my head out at least once a day, if nothing else."

The process of adjustment takes time and is often a period of anxiety (Van Maanen, 1978). At first, in the company of others who are new, one's sense of aloneness can increase. Smith and Berg (1987) contended that:

> People are often driven to join a group or stay in one to deal with their loneliness, yet the group experience often makes them feel more lonely. The bind for members of a group is that the group stirs their oceanic fears of being swallowed up, with the attendant possibility of losing their identity, their autonomy, their own personal boundaries. (p. 42)

It is not unusual, then, for new residents, like Josh, to keep physically and emotionally distant from others:

> The first week I didn't allow them [other residents] to make me feel no kind of way. I isolated myself in my room basically 'til I got used to being here. I had to get used to the place in order to make it my home . . . and then I slowly started to come out and talk with other people. I would speak and when they asked certain questions, I would say it in such a cold way that they would stand far away from me and be careful with what they say. I kept it like that for a while.

Residents, however, have the simultaneous desire to separate from and integrate into group life. Smith and Berg (1987) argue that "the simultaneous desire for inclusion and fusion triggers the fear of consumption, absorption, and deindividuation, while the desire to be independent triggers the fear of exclusion, aloneness, and isolation" (p. 66). Hardin, who had been in the house for 3 weeks at the time of this interview, expressed the everyday tension he felt in adjusting to so many people. "I say, 'Good morning.' . . . Sometimes I feel I don't want to say nothing to nobody. I just want to go down and get my glass of milk and make my eggs. Or I'll want to go down just to be around people for 20 minutes or 10. Like I say, I'm new in this setting, and just checking it out."

We find that the time frame for easing into the house routines and becoming comfortable with group living is anywhere from 2–3 weeks to 3 months. Forcing social participation too soon may put undue pressure on new residents to socialize beyond their comfort zone and can have detrimental effects. Janet, who took 4 months to decide whether to move in, because of her concern about living with so many people, looked back on her entry experience at BH 10 months before her interview:

> I'm less engaged now than I was when I first got here. At first, I did try to interact a lot more, but I felt that I was being forced to do a lot of different things I didn't want to do. It was extremely uncomfortable, unnatural . . . the activities, the movies. There was too much togetherness for me. I felt [you had to be] too attached to a group, having to act and react as a group. I'd always liked being an individual.

Janet learned ways to control her social distance: "Eventually, I was able to find more of a middle ground where I can feel comfortable. I go down to meals now. If I don't want to sit at a large table, I can sit at a table where there are just two or three other people."

A major exception to the more passive strategies associated with keeping a low profile is the entry experience conveyed by Tyler, an extroverted, upbeat, and humorous person (see portrait in chap. 4). Initially, he tried to keep a social distance, but, as he told us, his more gregarious nature only needed an invitation:

> My first evening, I was going to sit down at a table by myself, mind my own business, and not bother anybody. Cassey [another resident] says, "Oh no, we won't have that here," and he pulls up a chair. Instantly, I felt like family. Sonja was eating like a bird. I treated her like a child; it was a time that she needed it. She said something about being through eating, and I said, "Oh no, you need to finish your pasta and eat two more bites of chicken." She did. It was instant acceptance, although Cassey did say that maybe there wasn't enough room in the house for the two of us, 'cause we're both gregarious little "girls," very good at camping it up.

The emphasis in socialization is generally biased toward the larger unit: "The individual is expected to 'fit into' the larger social unit . . . we don't hear much said about 'individualization,' the process by which the individual . . . affects the social order, perhaps even modifying or transforming it" (Christensen & Cheney, 1994, p. 226). Our observations and interviews at BH suggested that individuals attempt to modify the social order, but occasionally they fail miserably. These take-charge innovators, who possibly have a high need for control, are often frustrated by lack of support for their ideas and/or their interactional style. Barry, an ex-high school class president, and an action-oriented individual, entered BH highly motivated, offering new ideas and leadership to the community. Three weeks after being at BH, he described a significant change he helped institute and the resistance he encountered: "I'm an organizer type. I created a resident committee with a [resident] 'head of household' each month . . . to mediate between residents and staff . . . but I just ran into a great deal of apathy."

The turning point in Barry's entry experience was the demise of the talent show he spent weeks trying to organize. Soon after this failure, he found himself spending more time in his room or outside the house. As Barry's experience shows, newcomers must learn about and adjust to the power and politics of the organization if they intend to assimilate (see Chao, O'Leary-Kelly, Wolf, Klein, & Gardner, 1994). At BH, where the norm for newcomers is to keep a low profile if they want to be accepted, those who try to exercise leadership too soon may find a lack of support. For Barry, who wanted to be "in charge of my own destiny," the combination of structural constraints and resident apathy made life at BH intolerable. He soon moved out of the house.

❋ ❋ ❋ ❋ ❋ ❋ ❋ ❋ ❋ ❋

Coping with expectations, confronting diversity, learning the ropes, and participating in shared organizational identity pose cautious beginnings for most newcomers and challenges for veterans, whether in corporate or residential settings. But at Bonaventure House, these issues are secondary to the overriding reality that residents are facing the last few months and years of their lives. Neither newcomers nor veterans can afford the luxury of a prolonged, agonizing entry period if they are to get on with the business of living together with AIDS. Stability and comfort must soon be found in emotional connections and in the enduring routines of everyday life.

3

The Fragility of Relationship:
The Social Dynamics of Everyday Life

Portrait of Rob

Rob had been a resident at BH for 7 months at the time of our initial contact with him. He saw himself as the "loner type," but, at the same time, volunteered for various house activities. He enjoyed contact with residents the most when they were "sitting there kind of quiet . . . [because] I can channel their whole outlook into something that is more positive. . . . I get a big high out of that." Rob found conflict, what he called "negative forces," very disturbing, and tended to stay to himself for his own protection. In the following passage, he shared an interesting dilemma in trying to mark his social boundaries:

> Some people have their doors open all the time. I see that as an invitation that says, "Come on in, I'm lonely in here." Now if I get in a mood where I'm tired of sitting around in my own little shell, I'll come out. I'll go downstairs, but in my personal surroundings I'm not one to visit other people's rooms or have them visit mine. This is my castle. It's my personal space . . . where I entertain my visitors from the outside. It's my world, so I want it to be personal. A coworker [outside BH] gave me one of these "Do Not Disturb" signs. I haven't used it yet and I was debating whether I really should, 'cause I don't want to make a statement like "Leave me alone." I don't want to say that and then have them shut me out altogether.

Portrait of Clyde

Clyde had been at BH only 3 weeks at the time of our interview, and although he suffered from epilepsy, mild dementia, and severe nerve disorder in his legs, he was incredibly upbeat and positive. He was a student of psychology and a science fiction buff; he even described how his epileptic seizures made him stronger, "like that scene in *Star Wars*; if you're destroyed, you come back a thousand times more powerful." His version of relationship formation at BH was rather contradictory and confusing, but nonetheless expressed how political and social spheres relate:

> I'm like a magnet to steel. I start to form allegiances. My first allegiances were not social here. This is strange, they were political. Now we're becoming more social. During some of the conflicts, everybody would come up to me and say, "I'm glad you said that." But they were more political. That's backwards. You're supposed to be socially connected to people first. You find out what a person's political beliefs are, how they feel about different things, how they feel about living at BH, how they feel about being negative or positive, and then you decide to not be close to them. If you believe in what he believes in, you have a political or philosophical oneness. That's one thing that I find holds people together more than anything.

Rob and Clyde's comments suggest some of the complexities and dilemmas in negotiating social life at BH. As with all interpersonal relationships (see Schutz, 1960), once newcomers' inclusion needs have been met, control and affection needs become the dominant concerns of everyday interaction. Although the intrapersonal dialectical tensions discussed in the last chapter do not disappear, control and affection needs give rise to a set of interpersonal and intergroup tensions that must be managed (Altman, 1993). As this chapter shows, the tensions associated with developing relationships while establishing boundaries and fusing the political with the social emerge at BH from the competing struggles among individual needs, group dynamics, and organizational structures. We first explore the everyday interactions that lie at the heart of intimate relationships and social life at BH. Issues of power, authority, and control that enable and constrain communal life are then examined. We conclude by focusing on the case of dish duty as a contested practice where the social and political dynamics of communal life are woven together.

WE FIGHT TO KEEP WARM

Residents learn quickly that the primary public space for both formal and informal gatherings is the dining room, which consists of approximately 10 round tables that each seat six to eight people. Here, hot coffee, cold drinks, and snacks are available around the clock, and the radio is usually playing. There is no TV (it is located in the family room upstairs), so interaction and conversation abound. At various times of the day or evening, people gather to play cards or engage in planned arts and crafts.

Residents are allowed to smoke in the dining room, as efforts to completely ban smoking in public spaces in the house failed, although several restrictions have gradually curtailed this behavior (e.g., only residents can smoke in the house, no smoking during meals or house meetings). The marking of physical boundaries as smoking or nonsmoking tables, in particular, influences clique formation. Edward, for example, would have liked to get to know fellow residents at the smokers' tables, but, unfortunately, could not bear the smoke and, therefore, said he never attempted to get to know them.

As with any group whose members live in close proximity, residents become attuned to each other's idiosyncrasies, especially their biological time clocks, enabling them to predict certain social patterns, such as when specific individuals will be in the dining room. Residents knew, for example, that a central figure in the house, nicknamed *La Reina* (The Queen), always came down for a snack after she watched the 10:30 evening news, and Miguel, who had problems eating, diligently came down for the "midnight coffee klatch." There is a liveliness that prevails late into the night, even at 2:00 in the morning, in part, because sleeping and eating disorders that result from illnesses and medications undermine normal patterns. Then, too, after 10:00 p.m., there are no staff, volunteers, or visitors around, apart from an evening supervisor, so the residents take on a feeling of ownership of the house.

The dining room also invites "core" socializers who simply hang out, drinking coffee and talking. Clyde referred to these people, including himself, as "the dining room hags." These residents are often confined to the house by illness and/or lack of funds, but some actually prefer to be homebodies.

As in other closely knit groups, gossip appears to be the thread that weaves and unravels social cohesion. Overall, most of the gossip seems harmless, such as "Did you see what *she* was wearing?" Barry, one of the residents, however, complained that because there is nothing for residents to do in the house, all they do is talk about each other. "Sometimes I'm just not in a frame of mind to go to the dining room and subject myself to idle gossip," said Randy. "On occasion, I spend too much time in my room."

Interactions in the public space of the dining room can become particularly tense and stressful at times. Rhonda spoke about a "verbal thrashing" she received from another resident there. Obviously, people have bad days, but there are days, according to Rob, when everyone is on the defensive: "I call it 'snapping turtleitis,' it seems like everybody's always snapping at somebody, but I guess that's supposed to happen in any type of community-living situation." Tyler explained that certain language is not appreciated, and that house members learn to adjust to others' expectations: "I used the word 'bitch' in the second person and she found it very offensive. She told me, 'Those are fighting words. Don't ever call me a bitch again.' I haven't."

Myerhoff (1978) provided a compelling description of fighting (e.g., cursing, naming, shaming, gossiping) among the elderly in a senior citizens center, where little issues easily turned into minidramas. Myerhoff argued that fighting practices exemplify "definitional ceremonies, contrived to allow people to reiterate their collective and personal identities" (p. 184). She went on to say:

> Anger is a form of social cohesion, and a strong and reliable one. To fight with each other, people must share norms, rules, vocabulary, and knowledge. Fighting is a partnership, requiring cooperation. A boundary-maintaining mechanism—for strangers cannot participate fully—it is also above all a profoundly social activity. (p. 184)

Myerhoff's chapter on group tensions is poetically entitled, "We Fight to Keep Warm." She identified a central paradox of these "ceremonial fights," whose purpose is "to allow things to stay the same, and to allow people to discover this sameness in the midst of furor and threats of splitting apart" (p. 186).

Residents at BH also fight to keep warm; interactional conflicts are both evidence of solidarity and displays of defiance in the face of so many losses. Steven, a resident, offered a compassionate interpretation of these conflicts:

> Some people can be very dramatic, and usually the problems are nothing major, but one or two of the people involved will react in a big way, and I can understand them. These people have lost their jobs and loved ones, maybe their home, maybe a lot of personal possessions. And then they're in an environment where they don't have a lot of things and you take away just a tiny little something and maybe a little bit of their control or whatever, and because they have lost so many things, they hold on so dearly to whatever they do have. It does become a big issue for them.

Quarrels are not only the stuff of interpersonal differences and discord, they are also an affirmation of caring. There is a poignancy to these social rifts as testimonies of survival—that life, however oppressive, is still engaged with a bang rather than a whimper. In contrast to this unsettling image of public life at BH, there are the more quiet and intimate moments in private.

BEHIND CLOSED DOORS: PRIVACY AND INTIMACY

When the demands of group life become too much, residents can always go to their private rooms to be alone. In the early days of BH, residents often kept their rooms unlocked and open, but that openness and atmosphere of trust changed over the years due to increased incidents of theft, which are a deep transgression against the community.

Although we are friends with several residents, they rarely invite us to their rooms, nor do we seek them there; we usually meet them in the dining room or outside the house. Because their rooms are rather small—barely accommodating a twin bed, dresser, and chair (see Fig. 3.1)—and are the only private space afforded each resident, infringing on that space displays a certain inappropriate intimacy—like visiting a friend's home and socializing in the bedroom. Private rooms are considered one's castle, and it is taboo to enter without knocking. Clyde described how his door signals social boundaries: "I usually have the door open because we have a very nice floor. It's like a code. If the door's open, you can come and say 'Hi.' If the door's closed, that means someone may be ill or sleeping."

These comments hint at how socializing is facilitated by having approximately six to eight rooms on each floor, a plan that apparently allows subgroups to emerge. A number of residents spoke about the closeness on their floor, which they may sometimes create by moving or recruiting others to belong to a particular floor. After 5 months at BH, Charlotte felt this special bond; "I love living on my floor because I've gotten really close to the residents here. We understand each other, and take care of each other. We have our own little family. If one person is feeling bad and I want to go out, I'll make sure someone is there to look after him or her."

Although such bonds are common, we rarely detected, in our early days at BH, the presence of close, physically intimate relationships. This is due, in part, to a rule in BH's Policy Manual for residents that prohibits sex in the house (there is also a rule about no overnight guests), a rule that perhaps discouraged

FIG. 3.1. Each resident has a private room, although he or she shares a bathroom with another resident (referred to as a "johnnymate"). Private rooms are considered one's castle; one must knock and be invited to enter (photograph by Paul Merideth).

open expression or even discussion of romantic relationships. Although it is taboo, occasionally we heard of a house romance or the desire for one. In an interview with us, Simon talked about his deep loss over his partner's death a year earlier, noting that he sent a Valentine's Day card this year to his partner's last address, in spite of knowing that it would be returned, and lights a candle every day as a memorial gesture. "Residents as a whole want a monogamous, commited relationship," he said, "to be loved." Perhaps Simon was speaking of his own deep-seated desire, for 2 years after this interview, he found a profound and commited relationship with a new resident. Simon's partner spoke to the depth of this relationship, which they both realized may be their last:

> I wasn't expecting or looking for it. It was really wonderful and nurturing. We bantered and sparked for a couple of weeks, and then we started seeing each other ... and discovered we had a lot in common intellectually and emotionally. It didn't take very long for us to realize that very possibly this was an important and significant relationship. We've talked about it on several occasions, and we've both decided what we want is for this to be our last relationship. That could possibly sound a little morbid. It is not because we have HIV, but because we want to spend the rest of our lives together, however long that is.

They kept their relationship discreet, until Simon, a leader and long-term resident in the house, decided to out their relationship at a house meeting. According to Simon's partner, this revelation initiated a more open atmosphere for acknowledging and discussing romantic relationships in the house.

Romantic relationships, of course, are not without problems in community living. One couple, who ran hot and cold, often forced other residents to endure loyalty tests during their frequent spats, creating tensions and repercussions in the larger community. Simon's partner, whose sensitivity may have been more developed than most, was acutely aware that their relationship might provoke feelings of exclusion and loss in other residents:

> A lot of people have a tenuous hold on hope here. People, after an AIDS diagnosis, feel like it is impossible to have a relationship because nobody wants to deal with their mortality or because they don't deserve a relationship because they were stupid enough to wind up with AIDS in the first place.

Romance, love, and intimacy embody some of our deepest yearnings and most profound sources of happiness, regardless of when and where they occur in the course of our lives. But at BH, romantic relationships arise in a unique context fraught with many perils. Even though both partners have AIDS, there remain many physical threats to compromised immune systems in the exchange of bodily fluids, germs, and bacteria that accompany close physical contact and sexual activity. There is also the imminent death of one of the partners and the emotional coping that the surviving partner will face. Then there is the immersion of the budding relationship in the semi-institutional context of BH, where some staff and residents are uncomfortable with romantic, including premarital and homosexual, relationships. Relationship surveillance, whether real or imagined, by both staff and residents adds to the pressure to remain covert about engaging in romantic and/or physically intimate relationships, which is especially difficult for couples who like to engage in public displays of affection. Keeping a relationship secret is no easy task in a setting where residents are in such close proximity—where even in private rooms "walls speak."

Romantic relationships at BH speak of hope amidst constraint. Perhaps this is why a fellow resident, touched deeply by the openness of the relationship between Simon and his partner, slipped a note under Simon's door that "was just singing our praises—how wonderful it [the relationship] was and that he wanted to wish us the best."

SOCIAL SUPPORT: THE TIES THAT BIND

Intertwined in everyday gossip, spats, and romances are gestures of social support that range from simple to profound. B. H. Kaplan, Cassel, and Gore (1977) defined social support as the "gratification of a person's basic social needs (approval, esteem, succorrance, etc.)" (p. 50). Such needs are satisfied through social interaction with others; hence, as Albrecht and Adelman (1987a) argued, social support is best conceptualized as a communicative, symbolic act.

Social support in the form of practical assistance abounds at BH. When asked how residents help each other, Vincent, a 3-year resident, said, "Making sure that everybody's down for dinner. Making sure everybody at dinner has something to eat, if they can't get up. . . . I think those small gestures are really hard for some people to do. . . . Might be the most they can do." When residents are missing from dinner, people ask about them, and, if they are sick, a resident, volunteer, or staff member makes sure they get dinner. Nearby stores or take-out restaurants also afford ample opportunity for healthier residents to offer practical assistance to those who are homebound.

Practical assistance, however, goes far beyond serving people dinner or going to the store. Josh described how he actively tries to help other residents: "I helped one resident get undressed and into the shower. Once in a while, when people go in for their first chemotherapy treatment, I go with them." It is not uncommon for residents to pair off and develop friendships that become caregiver relationships—like having a guardian angel—or what Tyler, a resident, called "tandem relationships" (people looking after each other). Tim Budz, the Executive Director, told of a resident who slept at the foot of the bed of another resident to assist during a bout with an illness.

Emotional support is readily available, for residents know that someone—a resident, staff member, or volunteer—is at BH 24 hours a day to listen to problems, and, in many cases, to help deal with confusion, or ease anxiety and depression. Terrance described the support he got from fellow residents when he heard that Phillipe, his close friend, had just died: "When I heard P. died, I just broke. I went to my room and when I turned around there were people behind me. . . . There's always a door I could knock on. A lot of people have told me, 'If you need to talk, just knock on my door.' That means a lot. It's some place I can always go and talk."

In some cases, it is the perception rather than the reception of social support that is most critical (Albrecht & Adelman, 1987a). Kenneth, a resident, said, "Support has been there, but I've always pulled away. I haven't sought it. I think sometimes just knowing it's there if I wanted it makes me feel good."

It is naive, however, to believe that social support always is helpful. Many scholars contend that there is a dark side to social support, arguing, for example, that reliance on others for support often does not help a person's self-esteem and may even produce the opposite effect by promoting learned helplessness (see Adelman, 1989; Albrecht & Adelman, 1987b; Albrecht, Burleson, & Goldsmith, 1994; Chesler & Barbarin, 1984; La Gapia, 1990; McLeroy, DeVellis, DeVillis, Kaplan, & Toole, 1984; Rook, 1984; Wortman & Lehman, 1985). The benefits obtained from social support may also come at a price, as reflected in the qualifier "no strings attached" or the common expression "the ties that bind." Abdel-Hamlin (1982) thus referred to social support as a potential mixed blessing.

Researchers, however, typically frame the positive and negative sides of social support as either–or, referring, for example, to such principles as benefits versus costs. Social support, consequently, is seen as positive when the rewards outweigh the costs. This assumption is flawed because it treats social support as a duality rather than a dialectic. Our experience, observations, and interviews show that social support at BH is riddled with subtle and overt *coexisting* tensions for both providers and recipients. That is, the relative benefits and detriments of certain actions depend on who offers support, who needs support, and so forth. These tensions are revealed in the acts of mutual caring in coping with AIDS, including providing information about symptoms and medications, helping versus pampering, trying to save face, expressing concern and affection, creating opportunities to reciprocate support, diagnosing mental illness, and determining whether someone is sick enough and needs social support.

Residents often speak of the supportive information they get from one another regarding their illness, medication, or social services; from their peers, residents gain information about such divergent issues as seeing a neurological specialist and obtaining discounts on local bus services. Residents often turn to each other or the staff for advice about how to interpret symptoms, deal with complex side effects from medications, or use available technology and equipment (e.g., catheters). At one dinner conversation, a resident obtained several opinions about which food supplement would best bolster his diet without causing diarrhea. In providing such information, residents serve as communication brokers (Adelman, 1989) and a lay referral system (McKinlay, 1973), directing others to medical care and helping them stick to a medical regimen.

Informational support, however, can be problematic. Lay information can be a matter of pooled ignorance, producing an intervention that results in misdiagnosis and delayed treatment. One resident with a skin rash was unofficially diagnosed with scabies because there was an outbreak at the house. Elaine commented on fellow residents' tendency to "just turn around and say, 'That's what it is,' and I don't think they really know what it is. . . . They [those with symptoms] should be going to their doctors."

Another dilemma is walking the fine line between helping and pampering. Complaints by residents suggest that the climate of support can turn to intolerance if, in Elaine's words, fellow residents are "letting themselves be waited on." Branden claimed, "Everyone wants their own private slave. They think they're dying and they can behave any way they want." Maria, another resident, noted, "We don't have a lot of sick people, we have a lot of lazy people. They don't want to do shit." The Executive Director believes that, for some, AIDS is their claim to fame, providing a glorified identity and an overstated sense of entitlement—"I'm dying, so give me."

New volunteers and staff often do not recognize the difference between social support and overindulgence because they are too eager to help. Kenneth, a resident, "feels very useless; it's almost as if at times they [volunteers] don't want you to do anything. They'll do it for you. Some have been very patronizing, which I don't like at all." Pete, who must use a wheelchair, shared his dilemmas in rejecting well-intentioned help:

> There's quite a few that will get things for me. Sometimes it's irritating because they're constantly asking if I want something. I feel bad enough that a lot think I can't do it on my own. I've always been a very independent person. Like the other morning, I had three people come up to me and ask me what I wanted for breakfast. Usually, I have a cigarette, do my medications, and then decide what I want. I snapped at the third person, a nurse. I said, "When I want something, I'll ask for it." The following morning, I apologized to her and explained the situation.

The issue of dependence, in part, reveals the importance of, and threats to, saving face. Goffman (1959) defined *face* as the self-image that people project in interactions, but it is also an image that is supported or can be threatened by others, as in the case of embarrassment. Goldsmith (1994) claimed, "No matter who the supporter, no matter what the need, no matter what kind of support act is performed, face threats and face wants are a pervasive feature of supportive interactions because they are a pervasive feature of social life" (p. 36). Her review of face-saving literature provides evidence that "saying the right thing" does not come easily. Well-intentioned messages may inadvertently be perceived as intrusive or make the recipient look weak, increase stigmatization or loss of control, or threaten autonomy.

At BH, a seemingly innocent inquiry about another's health, a common greeting ritual in everyday interaction, can be a problematic form of social support, revealing the "communicative properties of socially constructed assistance" (Adelman, 1989, p. 32). Repeated, genuine inquiries to someone who has been sick, like "How are you feeling?," although expressing concern for the other's well-being, may be viewed by residents as unwanted solicitousness. Tyler described this bind:

> Sometimes people are entirely too solicitous for each other's comfort. That's one of the horrible symptoms for caring for each other—worrying about you too much and letting you know about it. Worry about me all you want, just don't ask me how I'm doing every 3 minutes. Sometimes we need someone to voice their care and solicitation, but it's a very hard thing to balance.

> Sometimes you can work someone into a frenzy . . . with that much solicitation. . . . Like if someone comes downstairs, and you say, "Ah, you look sick, what's wrong with you? Are you coming down with something?" Before the day is out, if enough people say it . . . they're convinced.

Expressed concerns about another's health present an interesting dilemma whereby such supportive gestures can be interpreted as intrusive and inadvertently deflate rather than bolster self-esteem. For those with life-threatening or chronic illnesses and/or disabilities, too much support may simply reinforce their sick role (see Cawyer & Smith-Dupré, 1995; J. D. Fisher, Goff, Nadler, & Chinsky, 1988; R. M. Kaplan & Toshima, 1990).

Conversely, complimenting another on her or his appearance might bring beneficial results to the person being addressed. Tyler continued with an example that results interestingly in a more positive effect of solicitation:

> I think the obverse of that is, one day Antonio came downstairs, and I said, "Antonio, you look really good," and he said, "I was just telling everybody I was feeling like shit, and here you are telling me I look good." "Yeah, you look well-rested and everything." "Well, I slept two hours last night." "Well, you still look well-rested, so don't worry about it." He had a much better day because someone thought he looked well-rested. . . . Mind over matter—if you don't mind, it don't matter.

Even simple gestures of affection are not without problems, as they require sensitivity to personal preferences and knowledge about a person's health status. For example, the Brothers at BH are known for always giving hugs. Charlotte spoke of these affectionate, paternal hugs: "When I get up in the morning or go downstairs, Brother C. hugs me and kisses me. That brightens my day. It's like he's taking the place of my father. Same with Brother M." Vance, however, found all the hugging initially "kind of awkward . . . because these were people I didn't know. I don't feel that way anymore. Now, I do it myself." Trace, a very affectionate man, prefers to give his consent: "Too much hugging . . . that bothers me sometimes. I ask people, 'Can I have a hug?'" Apart from personal preferences, certain physical problems make this gesture off-limits, such as when residents have a contagious skin infection, find hugging physically painful, or are wearing a heart catheter.

Social support is also problematic with regard to saving face when it increases feelings of dependency and threatens autonomy. In the course of volunteering, we learned how to offer support in more indirect ways so as to decrease the sense of dependency that often accompanies feeling ill or being disabled; strategies of indirect assistance include diffusing the assistance and providing opportunities for reciprocity. At dinner, for example, we asked everyone at the table rather than just a disabled individual, "Does anyone want something?" When we left the house after volunteering, we often asked residents sitting in the dining room whether anyone needed a ride in the direction we were going. When we brought videos to the house, we made sure that a resident was in charge of returning them to the store, thus saving us another trip and permitting an opportunity to thank him or her for the favor. When Trace, a very religious person, was quite ill, he asked Mara to read him a special passage from the Bible. Because she was unfamiliar with the passage, she sought his help in understanding it, a request he enthusiastically appreciated.

Residents, too, know the value of offering support while ensuring some form of reciprocity. As noted earlier, residents differ in financial status; it is not uncommon for the "haves" to assist the "have nots," but in ways that promote reciprocal support. As Tyler explained, "Some of us are better off financially, so we'll say, 'I'll buy you a hot dog if you go over to [name of store].' So little social interactions are thinly disguised charity." He described how Sonja, an older, maternal woman, used her interpersonal skill and intuition to promote reciprocity:

> Sonja is another catalyst for community. She comes across as very needy and very strong at the same time. Sometimes her strength is to know when she needs something. For instance, a couple of times when Sam really needed to be needed, subconsciously Sonja knew to need something from Sam at that time [i.e., asking him to go to the store for cigarettes]. In needing his support, she was supporting him. She's actually very good at that with a lot of different people.

One condition resulting from AIDS that poses special difficulty in offering social support is dementia, which results in confusion and forgetfulness. There is no doubt that residents feel deeply for those disoriented by dementia. Clyde appreciated the emotional support he received:

> Sometimes I have problems with mild dementia and a little bit of confusion. It's nice to be able to come down here in the middle of the night and talk to someone to get my bearings. It's like a computer; I get a little confused, like I dumped all my programs. Sometimes I go through various depressions too, and depression for me is a very deadly thing. Many times I come down in the middle of the night for cereal and I'll stay and talk to people. That's the incredible part about being here.

There are times, however, when a resident engages in forgetful or bizarre behavior, and the tendency is to dismiss it simply as a symptom of dementia. According to Edward, fellow residents often conclude "that someone has dementia, I don't always think that. I think there's a lot of reasons to be confused; sitting here all the time, they may be in bed all day. I don't think it's necessarily dementia all the time when people forget things. Everybody forgets things."

Confusion about whether someone has dementia is particularly painful when it is misdiagnosed and social support, consequently, is not offered. Branden remarked about the lack of sympathy shown to a resident who "didn't know whether he was coming or going. People moaned, groaned, and bitched at him and made his life hell. I was thinking, 'Don't they realize he has dementia?'"

In a similar vein, there is the question of whether a resident is sick enough and needs social support. Because many AIDS-related symptoms are not visible, a person can appear healthy and robust, but still feel ill. Barry, for example, was a burly, strong-looking resident who appeared healthy and was an independent type who, in his words, liked to "take the bull by the horns." Yet, his physical suffering and need for support were very real:

> I appear outwardly to the world as being fine. To look at me, you wouldn't know I was sick. There's a little disbelief that there's really something wrong, that I'm really dealing with any issues. I've had problems because I have KS [Karposi's sarcoma, a form of cancer] in my rectum and I've had severe pain related to that. I think that when they saw me suffering in the same way they were, I think it eased a bit. They realized I'm not as healthy as I outwardly appear.

Social support can be a simple gesture, but it can also be a rather complex exchange that entails concern for saving face, insuring reciprocity, and an accurate interpretation of symptoms and genuine need. Efforts to bolster a person's image or state of mind can backfire, with negative repercussions for both parties. Moreover, the symptomology of AIDS can be bewildering, creating numerous dilemmas for interpreting and responding to one's own or another's illness. Mara, for example, complimented Enrique on his gorgeous, dark tan, whereupon he replied, "Oh, that's due to kidney failure." According to another resident, Maria, this type of compliment is a common mistake. Obviously, situational knowledge, in this case about AIDS symptoms, is absolutely crucial for helpful, supportive communication.

Although there is low tolerance for negativism, whining, and "drama queens," there is surprisingly high tolerance and concern for what residents deem to be genuine distress and deviant behavior arising from living with AIDS. We recall seeing a resident who was extremely agitated and making a scene. Another resident patiently told us that the former was upset because he had just learned that his T-cell count had dropped dramatically, a sign that his illness was advancing rapidly.

We have witnessed the acceptance of numerous individuals by the members of BH, such as Mannie, the racist resident who turned around (discussed in chap. 2), and observed incidents that would probably not be tolerated in most social circles, regardless of the explanation. There is deep compassion and acceptance in the house, although limits to prolonged or highly disruptive behavior exist as well. When normative pressure and staff guidance do not alter problematic behavior, a resident may be asked to leave. Expulsion occurs most often, however, because of violations of house rules barring drug and alcohol usage. Since the house opened, approximately 40 residents have been asked to leave, and about 40 others have chosen to leave voluntarily.

FROM SUPPORT GROUPS TO HALLOWEEN PARTIES: BUILDING COHESION

Personal and collective problems that cannot be resolved in informal exchanges—whether trivial issues or major crises—are often addressed in the weekly support group (see Fig. 3.2). Although designed primarily to help residents cope with their illness and the loss of others, the support group is also a site where problems of group living are discussed. The group is facilitated by a staff member; according to some residents, the staff member's presence sometimes proves problematic because of his or her power and authority, but using an outside facilitator unfamiliar with house issues and policies was not considered desirable.

Outsiders are prohibited from attending the support group because discussions are confidential, so we were not able to observe these meetings. Interviews and questionnaire data, however, revealed mixed sentiments about this house practice. About 61% of residents surveyed participated regularly in the support group because it: provides them with emotional comfort (62.8%); resolves conflicts among residents (61.0%); enables them to cope better with their illness (52.6%); and helps them deal with the loss of fellow residents (52.6%). These findings are in line with theory and research that show support groups generally help individuals with similar problems normalize the effects of life crises by accepting their feelings of fear and anxiety, thereby achieving better mental health (see Gottlieb, 1988; Taylor, Falke, Mazel, & Hilsberg, 1988), and this is especially true for people with AIDS (see Cawyer & Smith-Dupré, 1995; Maione & McKee, 1987).

Residents who resent these group sessions complained that the meetings are primarily "bitch sessions" where a lot of venting and little problem solving occurs. Tyler said that he and other residents can predict what issues will be raised "in group" by all the rumblings that preceded it during the week.

The process of venting should not be underestimated, for it is an important source of emotional comfort because of the catharsis it provides. In fact, Zick and Temoshok (1987) found that emotionally sustaining forms of help were actually viewed by PWAs as more desirable and useful than problem-solving help. However, prolonged, repeated, and unresolved complaining without *any* problem solving can increase feelings of despair and hostility. A study of group intervention with PWAs by Fawzy and Wolcott (cited in G. F. Solomon, 1987) found that participants in unstructured emotional support groups had greater anxiety and were more likely to drop out than participants in groups that

FIG. 3.2.   Support groups deal with a wide range of issues, but focus primarily on coping with AIDS, the loss of residents, and the challenges of group living. Facilitated by staff in the family room, support groups are voluntary after the first 6 weeks of residence, and attendance varies depending on the issues that arise in the house during the week (photograph by Paul Merideth).

focused on problem solving, coping strategies, and education. The sounding board function of venting is thus most useful when venting helps resolve troubling and stressful issues that confront people with serious illnesses (Albrecht & Adelman, 1987b). As Wortman (1984) noted in relation to cancer patients, "Verbalizing personal concerns during a time of stress can help clarify feelings, to develop strategies for managing them more effectively, and to begin active problem-solving" (p. 2343).

Venting, combined with problem solving, in support groups is especially important at BH. Prior research tends to focus on support groups where members meet on a regular basis, but do not live together. BH residents, however, cannot just leave the support group meeting and go home; they are home. Although supposedly confidential, it is not easy to contain the support group and hold issues over until the next meeting. Invariably, issues overflow into daily life and become grist for the mill. As Jason, a resident, noted, "You still have to eat together." If the problems discussed in the support group are not dealt with successfully, the house is affected the whole next week by "who said what" in the support group. Thus, residents resent the support group when it is merely a "bitch session" and are less likely to want to attend the group the next week, whereas constructive meetings where feelings are aired and conflicts resolved have very positive effects on the quality of everyday life in the house.

Formal support groups at BH are also considered crucial for volunteers and staff. Professionals and volunteers who care for those with AIDS are extremely vulnerable to emotional exhaustion and burnout (see Cawyer & Smith-Dupré, 1995; Kelly & Sykes, 1989; Sosnowitz & Appleby, 1988), and support groups help caregivers confront the emotional highs and lows they experience (see Lehman, Ellard, & Wortman, 1986; Ojanlatva, Cochrane, & Walker, 1991). Staff members at BH are thus required to attend a monthly support group, and volunteers must attend a monthly support group for the first 6 months of volunteering, and are encouraged to attend thereafter.

Attending to the religious and spiritual needs of residents is another institutional form of social support. The range of pastoral services offered to those who wish them are designed to help residents, family, friends, staff, and volunteers manage spiritual well-being. Pastoral services are viewed at BH as "an important component of holistic care" (DiDomenico, 1993, p. 111), and offer an additional formal support system that helps address the existential questions the illness raises. Our surveys revealed that 62.7% of residents find that spirituality and/or religion helps them cope better with the illness, 54.2% find the spiritual and/or religious environment at BH very comforting, and 40.7% have become more spiritual and/or religious since arriving at BH.

Apart from meeting individual needs, spiritual practices also facilitate community development. Separate small groups meet for Bible study or to discuss the text, *The Color of Light: Meditations for All of Us Living with AIDS* (Tilleraas, 1988); additionally, residents attend various services held in the chapel, including morning mass, afternoon prayers, and Sunday services.

The only house-wide spiritual practices, offered spontaneously by anyone who volunteers, are saying grace before evening meals and an opening prayer at house meetings. The prayer may be religious or secular in content, ranging from a traditional recited prayer to acknowledgement of those in the hospital, special caregivers, or appreciation for food and health. Due to the religious overtones, however, this practice became contested. For some residents, the common prayer was seen as a forced institutional practice, whereas for others it was, in Maria's words, a moment to "be together . . .; [without it] the place is turning into such an institution." After heated house deliberations (discussed later in this chapter), this ritual is no longer practiced.

The moments when social cohesion are celebratory and the house truly comes together are at the numerous social events that punctuate religious and secular holidays, and the occasions for paying tribute to those who serve BH. The annual party to recognize volunteers is a celebration that residents and staff take great pride in planning, for it is a way of thanking the volunteers for all the support they have shown residents and staff. Yearly anniversaries of the opening of BH are marked by a formal dinner that many leaders of the Alexian Brothers attend. In 1994, for the first time, residents threw a surprise Recognition Party for the staff. Secular holidays, such as July 4th, and thematic parties, like Hawaiian luaus (see Fig. 3.3), often transform the more sedate atmosphere of the house into a festive environment through music, decorations, barbeques, and dancing. There are also smaller events almost weekly; birthdays are accompanied by a cake at dinner, video nights are held twice a month, special dinners are prepared by residents, staff, volunteers, or visitors, and field trips and free tickets to plays and events are sporadically available.

As with any group, planning social events does not always go smoothly. Getting residents together at BH can be a headache. Josh saw "some people around here as fuddy duds; they don't want to get involved in things or group activities or do anything fun." In addition to lack of interest, failing health of residents may prevent their participation and hamper the intensity of the collective experience. However, no matter how many residents attend the functions, our observation is that they truly appreciate these moments when the community spirit of BH percolates to the top.

The Halloween Party is an especially festive and cooperative event, a time when cross-dressing by males is the popular motif and liminality truly reigns. Carnivals and other playful rituals like Halloween, what Bakhtin (1965/1968, 1929/1984) called the *carnivalesque*, "allow parties to suspend temporarily their everyday, normal practices and personas in order to deal simultaneously with underlying oppositional tendencies from the relatively safe vantage point of their playful interaction" (Werner & Baxter, 1994, pp. 367–368). The Halloween Party is truly one of those opportunities, apart from the bereavement rituals (discussed in chap. 4), for the experience of *communitas* (Turner, 1969)—that is, when ritual strips away social impediments that divide and distinguish members and suspends social structure. This transformative experience occurs when members are "permitted to act spontaneously, without social responsibil-

FIG. 3.3.   In addition to celebrating traditional holidays, residents and staff work coop-
eratively to create novel parties. The Hawaiian Luau party held in the courtyard of the
Bonaventure House, pictured here, is a festive occasion where comunitas prevails
(photograph by Paul Merideth).

ity and accountability" (Myerhoff, 1975, p. 34). A good example is the 1995 Halloween Party, which featured a prize for the most out-of-character costume. But moments for communitas at BH are rare. The institutional nature of communal living is dampening and can result in dry periods during which the community has no "intense positive collective behavior experience to generate commitment" (Zablocki, 1971, p. 168). However, when residents gather off site for such events as the Gay Pride Parade, field trips to amusement parks, hay rides, the zoo, and spiritual retreats, fleeting moments of communitas prevail.

These transitory moments and celebratory events become the stuff of storytelling for weeks afterward, and they are recorded in the house scrapbooks (see chap. 4), revealing their lasting imprint. They are profound moments, not only because they offer escape from the structures and routines of collective life, but also because they suspend the shadow of AIDS and simply affirm the joy of living. As Myerhoff (1975) noted eloquently, in community, it is "the fluctuation between joy and duty that constitutes the ceaseless flow of social life. Getting stuck at either pole and neglecting the existence and importance of the other are fatal" (p. 35).

ENABLING AND CONSTRAINING:
POWER AND CONTROL

Group life is rarely a free-floating, unconstrained activity; social interactions are always expressed within the political structure that characterizes the group. As Poole, Seibold, and McPhee (1986) reminded us, "All groups are embedded in institutions—organizations, religious orders, interorganizational networks, legal systems, and so forth—which shape and constrain their actions" (p. 241). Whether communes or corporations, all institutional life demands negotiated order for survival (Strauss, 1982). The need for order leads to struggles for control and power that crystallize tensions between the individual and the group (Carbaugh, 1988a, 1988b; Katriel & Philipsen, 1981), autonomy and connection (Baxter, 1988, 1990; Baxter & Simon, 1993; Bridge & Baxter, 1992; Goldsmith, 1990; Masheter, 1994), and independence and interdependence (Bochner, 1984; Rawlins, 1983, 1989, 1992). As Mumby (1993) maintained, "Organizations are thus political in that the complex system of discursive and nondiscursive practices that make them up reflect the struggle to fix and institutionalize the dominance of certain groups and meaning structures over others" (p. 21).

The most obvious power struggle at BH is between residents and staff. Residential facilities have strong, established institutional patterns, with many of the important decisions being made by those in power (e.g., staff, Board of Trustees), whose authority is legitimated, of course, by other institutions (e.g., State of Illinois, Alexian Brothers of America). These institutional patterns, with their accompanying bureaucracy, role definitions, power distribution, and control over resources, make up the infrastructure that both supports and conflicts with residents' preferences.

A primary tension between staff control and residents' desire for autonomy revolves around rules and regulations. Rules are numerous at BH, but not all pose difficulties. For example, residents, like Scott, saw clear reasons for testing everyone for TB, a highly contagious airborne virus posing special risks to PWAs: "Somebody had it, and never took their medicine; that's like living in a death trap. Certain health precautions need to be taken and strictly enforced."

Rules for insuring the well-being of individual residents and the collective, such as TB testing, are rather straightforward and uncontested. Other rules, however, can be resented deeply by residents, especially those that impinge on privacy or expose personal behavior. For example, because BH is a home for recovery, strict rules bar drug and alcohol use. Pete, who liked to collect wine, understood having the rule for those in recovery, but thought it was an invasion of privacy for residents, like himself, who were not substance abusers and perhaps wanted to drink a glass of wine after dinner in their rooms. Staff also have the right to drug-test anyone who has been a substance abuser, no matter how long he or she has been clean. Maria, one of the residents, spoke angrily about this policy, "I haven't used drugs for eons, but every time I go out, I hate to come back, 'cause I say, 'Man, what if they drop [drug-test] me?' And it's not that I'm dirty—I don't want to go through that shit." Residents in recovery who refuse to be tested are asked to leave the house. Some rules are simply nonnegotiable.

Room checks are performed occasionally for the health and safety of the facility (e.g., to prevent infestation, check fire alarms), or, when warranted, to search for contraband. Residents accept this intrusion when it is necessary, although even the potential for violating private space can be perceived as threatening, and make residents, like Jason, angry: "I don't like people being able to come in my room when I'm not here just because they're staff members, or rummaging through things; . . . the first staff member I find going through my things, there is going to be hell to pay."

Other rules about personal behavior evoke mixed reactions, depending on how they are interpreted by residents. A rule as simple as signing in or out of the house can be seen alternatively as an intrusion or as a form of caring. Kirk, who was asked to leave after 3 months at BH, claimed, "I dislike signing in and out when you leave . . . I don't think it's any of the staff's business. I'm grown, and so are all the other residents around here." Conversely, Josh saw it as evidence of "a real general concern for each individual here," and not as a surveillance tactic.

When asked whether there were too many rules in the house, residents were split almost equally. Resentments over too many rules are common. Living with others, either as a couple or in a group, always involves rules, but, in most cases, these rules are implicit. In residential living, however, rules must be explicit to insure fairness. Unfortunately, they also seem to proliferate at an exponential rate, as complaints often become settled by instituting a new rule.

Resentments over rules also reflect the loss of independence that residents experience in moving in to BH. Rob said, "I'm more upset about the freedom that I lost and the fact that I have to live by rules. It's like living in my mother's house." Perhaps it is the parental attitude of some of the staff that residents, like Josh, resent most: "Staff really get off on being parental, being able to slap your wrists and say, 'Oh no, bad boy.'" Ironically, although BH was designed to assist independent living, Branden believed there was "too much structure for someone this independent. . . . They have rules here that are like military school or boarding school, and that doesn't make for a strong community." Kirk, another resident, said, "Home is where you feel in control, where you don't have to answer to nobody, like you have to do here, so this is not home."

Rules both impede and foster community; as in all organizations, rules reveal the delicate balance between creativity and constraint (see Eisenberg & Goodall, 1994). It is not surprising, therefore, that many residents believe that rules are absolutely essential for community living and gratefully accept the exercise of authority by staff. Vance said, "There have to be rules, otherwise it would be a madhouse. . . . They have to have rules to keep the harmony." Tom similarly claimed, "I think that we have to be particularly strong in enforcing policies because if we allow residents to do as they please, then it's going to get way out of hand. The staff is here to reprimand us for all our misdemeanors." Tom's statement points toward how rules, roles, and reprimands are coconstructed between residents and staff.

Many of the residents have had problems dealing with authority figures all their lives (e.g., police, doctors, social workers) and have learned either to skillfully manage or sabotage these relationships. Tim McCormick, BH CEO, appreciated this ability and cautioned against trying to impose an authoritarian social structure on residents: "What we have are people coming who have lived skillfully by manipulating systems, other institutions much wiser and smarter than we are. . . . We are at a strong disadvantage if we try to create a system to contain them." Although some residents try to beat the system of authority, others simply avoid interacting with staff, as Kenneth explained:

> They're staff, they're administration, so I think that created a barrier right way. I mean, I had nothing to share with them because an authority figure you don't usually open up to. . . . "You're staff, I'm a resident, we don't mix." It's like on a job where the little persons don't associate with management type of thing. You stay away, no socializing.

Perhaps one of the reasons some residents may be reluctant to open up to staff is the lack of confidentiality in sharing personal information. BH staff use a team approach to case management, which means they discuss everything relevant to each individual resident and reach collective decisions about how to help him or her. Hence, no issue is strictly confidential, including discussions with the Pastoral Director. As Fred, a resident, remarked, "If you told one staff member, you told them all."

Of course, sharing information and gossiping about staff among the residents is also popular. Furthermore, the informational flow between staff and residents is rather porous, as revealed in a humorous, albeit semidegrading, analogy by Tony, a staff member: "You know the residents are like the dear, faithful, old family retainers that you read about in romantic books—the butler, the upstairs maid. They know everything. You're not fooling them, believe me."

Although there are significant difficulties in the interactions between staff and residents, due no doubt to differential power and health status, these problems must be viewed within the broader context of the high-quality relationship that residents perceive between themselves and staff members. The vast majority of the residents we surveyed (74.5%) characterized their relationship with staff as "excellent," and, as Table 2.1 showed, residents have deep respect for staff as professionals, community members, and caregivers.

It is also a mistake to assume that the only power struggle is between residents and staff. Residents themselves become enforcers of rules, and this internal policing, according to Rob, sometimes makes BH feel like a prison. For example, to prevent a depressing nursing home atmosphere, residents are not allowed to wear robes in the dining room from 10 in the morning until 10 at night. Once when Rob went downstairs in his robe during the early evening, another resident said, "What are you doing? It's not 10 o'clock yet." Although contributions to everyday house maintenance (such as vacuuming) are voluntary, with the exception of dish duty (discussed later in this chapter) and cleaning bathrooms after use, residents often become frustrated and upset with those who do not contribute a fair share to house chores. Barry said, "If you ask people to vacuum, it's as if you asked them to fly to the moon."

Some residents contribute more than their fair share, but they may pay a price. For example, Rob, who is rather shy and seldom engages in much conversation with fellow residents, volunteered to clean the aquarium located in the living room, but eventually became frustrated because it turned into the sole point of conversation with other residents: "It's like I'm Mister Fish. I agreed to feed the fish and now everything is like fish, fish, fish, fish, fish. And with the funding of getting the tank cleaned and this whole thing, I was kind of on a fish crusade myself for a few minutes, but I had fish burnout. I can only go so far with an issue."

Because of problems in equity and internal power struggles, residents formed a 3-person committee, the Resident Council, to voice their concerns to administrators. Members were elected by majority vote for a 6-month term. Many residents said they initially had high hopes for this council, but the structure and process quickly proved disappointing; indeed, after a couple of years of existence at the time our surveys were conducted, only 47.5% of the residents thought it was helpful. One unexpected negative consequence resulted from the election of members to the council. As Executive Director Tim Budz explained:

The format of having residents elected was far too stressful for people. What really triggered us [to note the problem] is that the people who were defeated could not rebound from the rejection by their peers. . . . Remember that we have very fragile people coming into this building. And although it wasn't a vote about their popularity, that's what it came out to be.

Perhaps the turning point in the council's history was when it argued over whether to say a prayer before dinner. We could not observe the heated debates that occurred in the Resident Council meetings or the subsequent house meetings over the issue of prayer at dinner, although informal conversations with residents and staff indicated that it was a volatile topic. As mentioned earlier in this chapter, the debate essentially centered on whether this practice promoted community, as perceived by the more religious, Christian residents, or represented an intrusion of religious and/or spiritual practices on public space.

The decision was made to suspend this practice, but the debate certainly took its toll. According to Maria, an outspoken resident, "From that day on, people have said, 'That Resident Council ain't shit.'" Shortly after the dinner prayer was discontinued, the Resident Council was disbanded and replaced with a Resident Advisory Board that has a looser structure, is voluntary and open to anyone who wants to join (in Spring 1995, there were four members who serve a 6-month term), and holds open meetings that any community member can

FIG. 3.4. This weekly, mandatory house meeting provides an important opportunity for residents and staff to voice their concerns about the day-to-day affairs of the house. Becoming heated discussions at times, these meetings are closed to volunteers and visitors (photograph by Paul Merideth).

attend.

The weekly house meeting, which is mandatory and facilitated by staff, is where residents' concerns about each other and the staff are openly discussed (see Fig. 3.4). Originally, the house meeting was held on Wednesdays, which conflicted with off-site support groups required for those in recovery (up to 60% of the population at BH). Consequently, house meetings were not well attended. Moreover, during the early days of BH, the house meetings were run in a formal manner with a set agenda focused strictly on maintenance issues, leading Kirk, one of the residents, to claim, "I don't believe they should be mandatory. They only last between 20 and 30 minutes and the little shit they talk about, they could just get a memo and pass it around the room."

The staff decided to make some substantive changes in the house meeting. The first decision was to change the meeting day to Friday so as not to conflict with the recovery group meetings. Because house meetings are mandatory, this change resulted in a full house at the weekly meeting. The second decision was to change the dynamics of the meeting. No longer business as usual, the meetings were redesigned to discuss whatever topics most concerned residents and staff. If necessary, a voluntary emergency house meeting is called during the week to talk openly about an important issue (for example, when a rash of thefts occurred in the house).

Taboo topics or those confined to the support or recovery groups now began to surface during the house meetings. Interpersonal conflicts, house romances, relapses, and dismissals from BH were openly discussed. The Executive Director noted that they could now talk about the "elephant in the living room," issues that loomed large but were left unspoken. Both staff and residents, he claimed, came to understand that "the process is much more important than the content. It's less important to talk about the detail of things than the process." In essence, the meetings, according to Budz, became "a very large support group."

After only a few months into this change, 72.8% of the residents we surveyed found house meetings helpful. Clyde noted that these meetings allow residents to "discuss our business in more of a democratic setting," and Terrance said, "I think they're great. The only thing I disagree with is that we go over the same things at the meetings. I think things should be solved."

Power struggles also exist among staff members, who are not unanimous in their approach to health care and interaction style with residents. Staff members share the core values of the Alexian Brothers: partnership, compassion, holism, and mutual respect. These principles guide their mission and are evoked to help resolve struggles among residents, among staff, and between staff and residents. However, depending on one's model of health care, these values are expressed via very different practices. We turn to a detailed discussion of these conflicting models.

There are two dominant health care delivery models at BH, which staff members themselves refer to as the *professional agency model* and the *ministry model*. The professional agency model emphasizes maintenance of professional boundaries between staff and residents, whereas the ministry model emphasizes love, support, and close relationships with residents.

The professional agency model advocates strict personal and professional boundaries for staff and volunteers at BH, a context where countertransference and favoritism can have repercussions for residents and lead to burnout of staff and volunteers. Executive Director Tim Budz, who is trained in this model, noted that the "biggest dynamic is there's all this countertransference that happens between residents and staff," where anger about the illness and loss of autonomy is transferred to staff members (e.g., displaced aggression, name-calling). Another problem results if inequities in affection are shown by staff or volunteers to certain residents. This possibility is difficult to avoid, but perceived favoritism can be a sore point among residents, who feel the sting of exclusion and become jealous.

Professional boundaries are also considered a necessity for reducing the strain of resident–staff relationships due to the increasing pressure of job demands. Rapid growth in services, increased demand for documentation from various funding agencies, and financial growth from a $300,000 to a $1.1 million a year operating budget have resulted in time constraints and immense paperwork for staff members that affect their availability to residents. No longer is a staff member able to enjoy a leisurely chat with a resident without documenting it. The Executive Director summarized the strain: "BH has become a big business versus the family that we originally set out to be." Considering the burnout and attrition of professionals in AIDS-related agencies, BH's average staff tenure of 30 months demonstrates an exceptionally high retention rate.

The ministry model, alternatively, problematizes the concept of boundaries between residents and staff. Tim McCormick, BH CEO, who identifies himself with the ministry model, explained:

> Through the Scripture, particularly in the persona of Jesus, there's this boundary-crosser person. . . . There were none of these built-in parameters, and so there's this constant crossing over and breaking the paradigm that was established. It's really established by those in control, or who think they are in control. Are we in this mode of boundaries of social service delivery, which is good for a social service agency, or are we in a ministerial mode that says . . . love is unconditional and really knows no boundaries? Our mission statement is compassion and hope. Now, when you talk to residents, is that what they are perceiving or are they perceiving a maintenance of a life to comply to certain norms or structures of a bureaucracy?

Not surprisingly, conflict between staff members who adopt these different philosophies sometimes occurs, as encapsulated in the following incident. In BH's early days, there were two elderly Alexian Brothers and a Franciscan Brother who—unlike staff members—lived in the house. Available 24 hours a day, they were seen by residents who lived there during that time as models of compassion; residents, like Steven, spoke often of the Brothers' selfless devotion and the spiritual guidance and comfort they offered:

They tend to look at things from the residents' point of view. They dedicated their lives to helping someone and being kind, so I think they are a bit more understanding and more supportive [than other staff members]. I tend to believe in them a lot more and trust them a lot more. It's almost like their motives are more genuine.

From a professional agency perspective, important boundaries were crossed, residents were too dependent on the Brothers, and living in the house was not viewed as healthy because of the potential for burnout. According to the Executive Director, "As a social worker, my boundaries have always advocated against anyone living in the facility, but from the ministerial perspective, that's very much a ministry of presence." In another interview, he added:

I never agreed with the Brothers living here. I thought that was a bad idea because they didn't have a separate identity from the facility. I think of the toll that took. Every single [telephone] page, every single fire alarm that went off—they were never off-duty. I think that ultimately affects people's mental health.

After the two elderly Alexians died from forms of cancer, Budz felt the remaining Franciscan was "beginning to burn out," and suggested that he move out of the house, which he did shortly thereafter. Although Alexian Brothers still work at BH, none reside there.

The desire for clear boundaries expressed in the professional agency model certainly affects us as well. As mentioned in chapter 1, we were asked to give up our formal volunteer roles when we became researchers, and vice versa. We developed friendships with some residents, but because socializing with them outside of BH is discouraged, these relationships became clandestine. We are not alone. Boundary crossing in the form of private invitations to social activities outside BH are not uncommon between residents and volunteers, and even some staff. We also take advocacy positions on behalf of residents, for we believe strongly in social-action research. On one occasion, a resident whom we considered a friend was asked to leave BH against her will because some administrators genuinely believed that she would be better off living independently. She formed a 3-person support team to mediate this conflict and chose Larry as one of the members. This put him, for a time, in an adversarial relationship with these administrators, but the meetings did result in a mutually agreed-on, 2-year plan for her to leave the house.

At the root of all the institutional practices of power and control discussed previously is the disciplining of residents, staff, and volunteers alike. Discipline, according to Foucault (1979), is an inherently communicative construct; power becomes concrete through discourse and discursive systems (see Mumby & Stohl, 1991). According to Sennett (1980), these discursive systems are both enabling and constraining. Barker and Cheney (1994) elaborated, explaining that disciplinary discourse systems are "'enabling' because they allow us to create reality in concert with others and, simultaneously, 'constraining' because the disciplines shape our behavior in directions that are functional for the organization" (p. 30). Paradoxically, as Smith and Berg (1987) contended, whereas "boundaries that contain," such as disciplinary discourse systems, normalize individual and collective behavior, they are the "very processes experienced as structures that create the anxiety in the first place" (p. 106). Because many of the structures and micropractices of discipline occur at the most mundane level (Foucault, 1979), we turn to a daily chore that weaves together the social and the political: dish duty.

DISH DUTY:
RESISTANCE AND COMMITMENT TO COMMUNITY

Social practices lie at the heart of community, but some are more contested than others. Contested communal practices are *pivot points*, where members' commitment to the collective is engaged, tested, and made public. Pivot points crystallize tensions between individual and group boundaries, as the contested social practice invariably demands some form of sacrifice by members. In her work on utopian communes, Kanter (1972) identified sacrifice (e.g., a vow of poverty) as a major mechanism for building community commitment. She cited Buber's (1958) description of the central role of sacrifice in constituting "a life in common": "[Sacrifice] is the community of tribulation and only because of that a community of spirit; a community of toil and only because of that a community of salvation" (Kanter, 1972, p. 134).

All communal life involves some form of personal sacrifice. Although residents at BH do not take vows, they engage in a weekly commitment, mandated originally by staff, to a "community of toil" in the much maligned and sacrificial task of dish duty. Once a week, a team of residents (usually 4–5) sets the tables for dinner, cleans up after the meal, and washes the dishes (see Fig. 3.5). In many respects, this innocuous yet deeply symbolic task compresses and reveals the dialectical tensions already described that comprise community life in general, and community life at BH in particular.

Doing dishes is a necessary evil. No matter in whose home it occurs, it is often a contested practice. BH certainly has problems getting residents to comply with dish duty, and various interpretive frames are used to explain residents' resistance, from differences in lifestyle to rebellion against authority, illness, and the BH community itself.

Personal lifestyle and laziness are common explanations for why some residents resist doing dishes. Scott, a resident who was contemplating moving out, in large part because of concerns over cleanliness, noted that those who do not do dishes are simply "lazy—I would hate to see if they lived alone what their sink would look like." Laziness is often attributed to improper upbringing. Jonathan, a newly-arrived resident, said, "Some of these folks never washed dishes . . . [and now] they feel that someone's bossing them: 'You're not my mamma.' . . . They never had to wash dishes, keep their house clean. I was raised different."

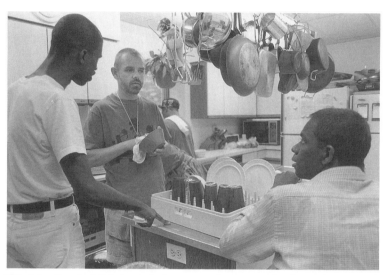

FIG. 3.5. Required dish duty is both a source of community bonding and a contested practice that produces much griping. This innocuous yet deeply symbolic task compresses and reveals the tensions that comprise community life at Bonaventure House (photograph by Paul Merideth).

Others' resistance to dish duty constitutes rebellion against the authority imposed on them. Dish duty becomes an extension of the power that staff have over residents, because it is assigned by BH administrators, who see it as helpful for building community. Many residents support this view, but not every resident agrees. Branden said he told the Executive Director "that if you think this kitchen duty is therapeutic, you've got another think coming." Many residents recommended hiring someone to wash the dishes, and the administration did hire three part-time people to assist.

A deeper, more problematic explanation for avoiding dish duty lies in residents' responses to their illness. As mentioned earlier, some residents use their health status as a reason to demand personal service; that attitude surfaces frequently when residents try to avoid doing dishes. Residents who are physically incapacitated, of course, are not required to do dish duty, but some, in the words of Maria, a resident, "are using this disease as an excuse. 'I can't go down because I'm tired.' 'I can't wash the dishes because I have the sniffles.' Man, you can have the sniffles and still do your duty." Jason, another resident, noted, "For some people, not doing dishes is a rebellion against their disease. They didn't want to be a part of this community. It is their way of fighting the world because you gave me this God-damned disease. It's just their way of dealing with the disease and that's very common."

Refusal to do dish duty is more than an act of personal defiance toward an unjust fate. For the collective, dish duty tests residents' commitment to community life and reaffirms interdependence. Whenever we helped with dish duty, we observed the camaraderie, joking, and concerted teamwork that accompany this task. There is little tolerance for freeloaders (e.g., those who are late, sloppy, or stingy with their duties), and failure to do dish duty results in a $25.00 fine. The fine, and its amount, was initiated by residents, but is collected by the staff, which places staff members in a precarious position, and, according to the Executive Director, leads new residents to see this sanction as being imposed by staff.

When the time arrives for monthly assignments, residents jockey to work on a good team and avoid those notorious for abusing their duty. Everyone, except the extremely ill or hospitalized, is placed on the dish duty roster, divided into teams, and appointed dates. The list is displayed publicly in the kitchen, a visual testimony to and reminder of each individual's obligation to the house.

As required teamwork directed toward house maintenance, dish duty fuses relational and governance practices. Moreover, because dish duty is the only required collective maintenance task, it is a popular topic of conversation and griping in the house. Katriel (1991) referred to the verbal ritual of griping as a major speech activity that helps to give "form and predictability to the domain of everyday informal relationships," and allows for an integrative topic for socializing in "communally approved ways" (p. 42). Her study among Israelis showed that "the proposition that griping produces solidarity was never contradicted" (p. 41).

Griping about life at BH is common. As Edward, one of the residents, said, "There's a lot of griping . . . it seems to me that the gripe is the central expressive genre that a lot of people have, and you certainly find that here just sitting around talking with people. I don't know why that is, except, of course, I guess people have anger." And nothing provides more grist for the mill than dish duty. As Tom explained:

> It was a major topic around here for the first month and a half that I was here. It was ridiculous. Every time someone opened their mouth around here, it was concerning dish duty. First I observed, and then I started contributing. Meetings were taken up by it. . . . Somewhere along the line, I stopped complaining about it.

Katriel (1991) noted that, unlike therapy, griping is an "antisolution" for addressing problems beyond one's control. However, griping about dish duty at BH serves the very important function of displacement—distracting residents from the more traumatic problems of coping with illness and death. Branden explained quite bitterly, "The underlying thing here is that we're all dying and that's not a real pleasant thought. No one wants to talk about that. They want to talk about missing kitchen duty. . . . That becomes the main focus once a week. That's all anyone screams about." Scott, upset about fellow residents who don't contribute, recognized that griping is not only a displacement of emotional distress but also a call for help: "I see individuals gripe about it [dish duty], don't show up . . . lie . . . just to get out of doing dishes and that makes me a little angry. Dishes wasn't the ace. Instead of me reaching out, saying, 'Is there any kind of way I can assist you?' or 'What really is the problem?'" And Robbin, who suffers from "massive dish burnout," acknowledged the positive aspect of griping for the community, but did not wish to partake in it: "The whole thing with dishes is just a dead issue with me. They don't have anything else to really focus on. I guess it's healthy for them to focus on the dishes. For me, I find it very boring, tiring."

Griping about dish duty offers not only a way of displacing feelings about illness and loss, but also serves—given the unusual and everpresent reality of living with AIDS—as a way of normalizing everyday life; it is a reminder that even in this bizarre trauma, one still washes dishes. People cannot live in perpetual crisis. Normalcy in everyday life, after all, is constituted in the accomplishment of and verbal protestations about mundane, trivial tasks. Paradoxically, the most legitimate excuse for not doing dishes is that due to illness, which is a harsh reminder of nonnormalcy (e.g., degree of sickness, disability, absence due to hospitalization).

This paradox is reflected in the ways support and sanctions are enacted for not doing dishes. We have seen residents assure those whose turn it was to do dishes, and who might come down to dinner but are too fatigued or sick to help out, not to worry about doing their duty. We have seen teams rally together and nonteam members help when official team members are absent due to illness. However, a major transgression in community life is to fake symptoms and use the illness as an excuse for not doing dish duty. To turn the illness on itself in this way is considered so offensive that the violator can be marginalized and even shunned within the community. In a strangely poetic way, these sanctions acknowledge the sacred—the respect for life and loss due to AIDS.

＊＊＊＊＊＊＊＊＊＊

Bonaventure House is a site of liminality, where life is linked to death, and residents are caught "betwixt and between." Amidst this fragility, members become closely connected to each other, in both solidarity and resistance. Turner (1969) noted that social life "involves successive experience of high and low, communitas and structure, homogeneity and differentiation, equality and inequality" (p. 97). Profound expressions of social support and messy disagreements of political strife test relationships and, in the process, create for residents a foothold in social life. It is this footing that ultimately prepares them for their final journey—together.

4

The Fragility of Loss:
Coping With Death and Bereavement

Give sorrow words: the grief that does not speak
Whispers the o'er-fraught heart, and bids it break.

—William Shakespeare

Portrait of Tyler

Tyler is a very camp, outgoing, and fun-loving person who is well-liked by fellow residents. He is profoundly introspective and articulate; his reflections reveal both the conflicting feelings and cathartic humor that often accompany the acceptance and denial of impending death:

> I can always be glad I built memories with so-and-so, but sometimes the anticipation [of death] is worse than the real thing. Sam [a fellow resident], for instance, wheedled his way into my heart from day one. He calls me "Haddie" because I've been had a lot. I think it's hilarious. Every time he tells it, he tells it like it was the first time and looks very pleased with himself. He made me fall in love with him as a person. He jokes that he's not going to be here much longer and asks, "What are you going to do at my balloon ceremony [a bereavement ritual discussed later in the chapter]?" He makes a joke of his mortality. I've asked him several times not to joke because I love him, but I know that someday he will die. But to hear it, to be reminded of his mortality scares the hell out of me because I don't want to go through the grieving process for Sam. I'd rather keep him around. There are several, usually the healthiest, who joke about their immortality and talk like

they are going to be here forever. Maria talks about how she'll be here 'til the cows come home. She said something about doing my quilt [donated to the AIDS Memorial Quilt]. I said she won't get the chance. What she doesn't know is that she started the competition to see which of us would have to do a quilt for the other. [Laughter]

⌐⁓⌐

Emotional attachments, coupled with ways of distancing one's self from the reality of death and dying, are embedded in the everyday interactions and more ceremonial events that occur at BH. This chapter focuses on residents' reactions to their impending death and the loss of others, the collective bereavement rituals that help bracket death, and the symbolism of material possessions and dispossession for both disengaging and remembering.

But first, we feel compelled to begin with a caveat to our narrative. In many respects, this was the most difficult chapter to write and it remains the most elusive. Death is imbued with so many myths, for "death marks the boundary of our knowledge, as of our lives; it is the definitive expression of our limitations as human beings" (Hawkins, 1993, p. 93). Our involvement with residents often left us grieving and heightened our sense of mortality. However, our feelings are but a glimpse of the profound loss that residents face almost daily. To avoid contributing to their distress, we often refrained from probing too deeply into residents' feelings about death or bereavement, unless they signaled a desire to discuss these issues. These personal experiences lead us to embrace Farmer's (1992) view that "research is very often an inappropriate response to suffering. In such instances, we may find that personal integrity *and* professional interest are best served by putting aside tape recorders and notebooks" (p. 315). Recognizing the delicacy of certain situations, we, too, set aside our tape recorders and notebooks.

Furthermore, although we attended numerous rituals and ceremonies for residents who pass on, we were not privy to the more intimate moments of bereavement that occur in support groups, private exchanges among residents, and conversations between residents and staff. As we know from our own experiences, mourning is intensely private, even when expressed in public. Although we address in this chapter the communicative practices that help community members cope with recurring loss, we recognize that treating the mourning of self and others as a collective experience does not do justice to their most private experience, even as we attempt to "give sorrow words."

THE DEPRESSION BIND:
WALLS, MIRRORS, AND THE PARADOX OF HOPE

The greatest threat to a community is the loss of its members (Kanter, 1972). Imagine, then, how fragile community life must be when, within a 6- to 12-month period, the majority of a community's members will die and be replaced by others. This impact is tempered, in part, by the "timing" of deaths. At moments, there is a felt reprieve at BH; months go by with illness, even hospitalizations, but no deaths. Community life feels stable, staff members speak about the house being healthy, and the trauma of loss is a strong but distant memory. At other times, the house experiences sporadic deaths, spaced intermittently, as though by appointment. Then there are the harshest times, when as many as six to eight deaths occur within a month. Barely able to recover from such losses, the chaotic disruption of community life is further exacerbated by a significant influx of new residents. Given this turnover, it is understandable that the house feels to residents, as Vincent said, "like a restaurant. How many times can you turn over a table? It's like, how many beds can you turn over?"

In a community residence where illness and death are constant features, coping with one's own illness is tied inextricably to coping with the loss of others. Residents are in a precarious position: they need to acknowledge their grief over the loss of others, but they cannot undergo a prolonged bereavement process, lest they themselves become sick.

Indeed, the relationship between psychological stress and physical symptomology—the mind–body connection—goes far beyond speculation; it is standard curriculum in contemporary courses in physiology. Stroebe and Stroebe (1987) explained the implication of stress due to bereavement, long considered one of the most difficult events in life (see Holmes & Rahe, 1967):

> There is now convincing evidence that relates psycho-social stress to impairment of immune functions as well as altered susceptibility to infectious disease (Jemmott & Locke, 1984). The implication . . . is that the loss experience is likely to be accompanied by alterations in immune functions which, in turn, lower resistance to infectious diseases and increase risk of morbidity and mortality from these causes. (p. 106)

Severe depression is a common reaction to the stress that results from loss, particularly in pathological or prolonged grieving. Stroebe and Stroebe (1987) went so far as to assert that depression from grief is itself a disease that can threaten the immune system.

PWAs, who already have fragile immune systems—especially those who live together in a group setting, experiencing much illness and death—must thus carefully guard against depression that could further compromise their immunocompetence. We refer to this precarious balance that residents face—the need to grieve while protecting one's health from grief—as the *depression bind* (Adelman & Frey, 1994).

Residents intuitively recognize this bind; in fact, we derived this notion from their own accounts in interviews of how they react to illness and the loss of others. Josh, a long-term resident, captured the essence of the depression bind when he described another resident's distress over the loss of a good friend in the house as "digging his own grave by being more and more depressed."

Overwhelmingly, these accounts reveal the problem posed by the desire to offer physical and emotional comfort coupled with not wanting to get too close to someone who will soon die, because of the pain that accompanies loss. Thus, what bonds residents into a community—illness and death—also tears the community apart.

Two powerful metaphors are expressed when residents speak about the difficulty of getting too close to someone who is ill or dying, even after that person has passed away: mirrors and walls (see Fig. 4.1). *Mirrors* refers to the ways residents identify with a fellow resident who is sick or close to death. Metaphorically, mirrors capture the reflection and projection of self in the illness and death of others, whether this be a positive reflection of seeing others as heroic role models (e.g., dying bravely) or a negative reflection of viewing tragic pain and suffering. "It's like looking at yourself," explained Jason. "You're visualizing that this is the way you might be in a couple of months, next week, tomorrow." Pete expressed the difficulty in continually being confronted by this mirror: "Death to me is just part of life, but since I know that could be me one day, it scares me. I don't want to see it. I don't want to be around it." Steven was even more blunt about seeing very sick residents, "I think it's throwing that death sentence that we all have in my face. I don't need to be reminded like that all the time. I know I have AIDS." It is, of course, impossible to escape the everpresent reminder of impending death in a residential facility for people with AIDS.

One of the ways residents cope with these often threatening perceptions and emotional reactions to seeing self in others is to separate themselves, both psychologically and physically, from those who are sick or dying, or from those who have died. *Walls* refers to the ways residents protect themselves from the psychological and emotional threats of illness, death, and bereavement of others.

Long-term veterans of BH (those who have been in the house for more than a year) are a distinct group because of their prolonged exposure to cycles of multiple deaths. Josh, one of the longest-term veterans, spoke of his gradual emotional detachment as a way of coping with what Kastenbaum (1969) called bereavement overload:

> Since I've been sick with this disease, I don't allow myself to become emotionally attached anymore, because in this business you have to let go constantly and you get used to letting go. That's important right now, because a lot of people go through depression when someone leaves and they really get sick. And I choose not to, and I hope that doesn't sound cold, but I choose not to, and I am pretty much happier and healthier that way. . . . And all the people that have passed away the last few weeks, man, it's good that I have. When they tell me that someone passed, I'll say, "Now they're resting in peace," and I go on. No more thought, no more nothing. I go on.

Vincent, another long-term veteran, not only distanced himself from relationships and bereavement rituals, but developed a vacation fantasy for those who never return:

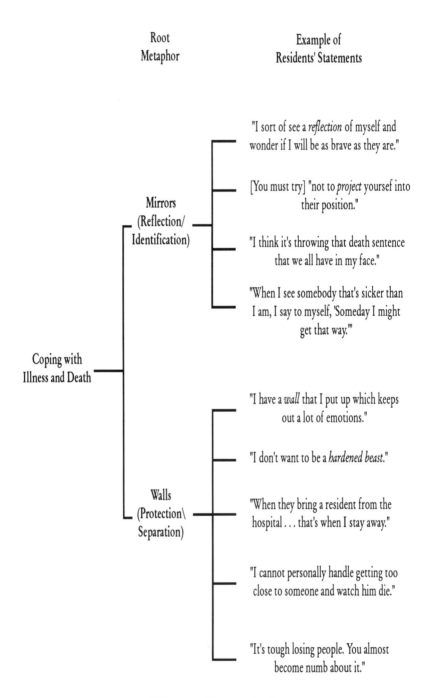

FIG. 4.1. Mirrors and walls.

I don't form that close of a relationship anymore. I've got my ready standbys, but to deal with all the losses is like, right now, my philosophy is I can't go to visit people in the hospital anymore. I can't go to too many wakes or funerals. If it was somebody I really did develop a relationship with, I, hopefully, will envision them on a vacation in sunny California or something like that, and I'll see them again someday and then they'll be back from vacation. I dwell on when I will see them. ... It's tough losing people. You almost become numb about it.

The construction of walls speaks to the elaborate containment of grief, a defense mechanism that helps residents cope with emotional overload. When his friend and fellow resident died, Clyde said he reached his "breaking point," which remains an unresolved issue because, "I'm afraid to experience the full range of emotions because emotions can be good and they can be bad sometimes." He provided a rich metaphor of emotional control:

Your emotions are like an 80-piece orchestra. Once you get all those emotions, like an orchestra in full play, you better know what you're doing because there's a lot of power and energy there. It can be a dangerous thing sometimes. My way of handling that is keeping it on a quartet basis. It would just touch me a little bit.

Clyde clearly recognized how easy it is to be overwhelmed, and employed his own version of what he calls "thought control and meditation to try to get over the rough parts."

Staff members, too, albeit in a very different way, struggle with walls and mirrors in their personal and professional relationships with residents, which is typical of residential settings, such as nursing facilities, where death is a common feature (see Collopy, Boyle, & Jennings, 1991; Hyman, Bulkin, & Woog, 1993). Staff members certainly are not immune to grieving for residents and confronting their own mortality, which is one of the reasons they have their own support group, but their response to death and dying is tempered by professional training that emphasizes maintaining healthy boundaries. Some staff consider boundaries and keeping distance to be synonymous, but Ann, a former BH staff member, critiqued this stance: "There are boundaries and then there is distance. I don't think it's the same. ... You can have good boundaries and do wonderful things for people and still maintain the relationship as a caregiver, but you can't do it with distance."

In a few cases, residents' desire for distance is reflected in their feelings about seeing fellow residents who are sick come down to eat or socialize in the dining room. Resentments about public displays of illness are voiced, for example, when residents with dementia begin to act inappropriately or when the extremely ill can only sit, almost comatose, sometimes blind, with their arms attached to an intravenous bag dangling from an IV pole. Branden said about these fellow residents, "They should do as much as they can do. I did not like seeing a catheter hanging out of L. at lunch and dinner. I did not like seeing P. come down." Residents who are extremely sick are often self-conscious, perhaps both because they do not want people to know and because they are a reminder to others, so they withdraw. As Brian shared, "I've gotten sick and very distant, to the point of just staying in my room. If I'm sick, I don't want to hang around the dining room. People have to look at me constantly and know."

Walls also occur in the physical distance that residents maintain from the illness of others. Fears over contagion are voiced when, for example, residents diagnosed with TB do not wear masks and cough heavily, or when a resident has exposed, contagious skin rashes. Vulnerability to infectious diseases makes these concerns salient to residents and adds to their desire to maintain physical distance, as Vance made clear even while helping another:

> I feel like I might catch something from someone who has been too sick or coughing too much. I helped a sick resident to breakfast, and fixed supper for him a couple of times. At the same time, I have this feeling or fear that I was going to catch some bacteria or something from him because I was too close. I walked him up to his room and I had to hold him. I kept thinking, "Can I catch it from being too close to someone?"

A major way distance is expressed is by avoiding visits to sick residents in their rooms or at the hospital. Josh talked about the stress and burden of hospital visits:

> Seeing someone on a life-support machine, they can't really talk, they're trying to write something out for you and you're trying to make it out. You're standing there. You can't help them, you can't do anything to make them feel better. All you can do is cry because you can't do anything. That pressure, that load that you get on your heart, can depress you. . . . Somebody here recently went into depression from going to see another resident in the hospital every day, and he had to go into the hospital himself. You don't have to go and see if you can't handle it. Don't go.

As volunteers, we too visited residents in the hospital; seeing their visible deterioration in this clinical setting is a vivid and haunting reminder of our helplessness.

Even Randy, who has a clinical background in medicine and assists fellow residents in improving their knowledge about AIDS, was shocked by all the end-stage people he found when he moved in to BH. He spoke of how distressed he became when he confronted the limits of his clinical interventions and had to bear witness to another's suffering:

> Initially, when I moved into the house, there were a lot of very sick people. I wasn't coping as well with my disease as I am now. It was a shock to be thrown into a situation where there were a lot of end-stage people who were very ill, confined to bed, not able to communicate well, and then being shipped off to a hospital. It was overwhelming in the beginning. I found it somewhat difficult to go to a resident's room, especially when the residents were Spanish-speaking. I felt at a loss as to what I could possibly provide for somebody who is extremely ill, bedridden, and did not speak English very well. Coupled with

the fact of the perceived emotional trauma of witnessing that situation, I preferred to avoid that to maintain my own level of well-being as a protective measure for myself.

Randy's comments lead to an important dialectical test for this community: the debate about whether those who are dying ought to remain at BH or relocate to a hospice or hospital. Some residents voiced resentments about the stress of letting residents die at BH, adamant feelings such as Branden's, "If you can't do for yourself, this isn't the right place. You need to be in a nursing home or a hospice." Such sentiments are rare, however. Overwhelmingly, residents believe that they have the right to die in their home (BH). As Charlotte noted, "I feel that if this is our home and if we wish to die here and have our last look at the house or be with our brothers and sisters, they [the staff] should grant us that wish." A less glorified response came from Kirk, a resident who felt that the right to die at BH is simply an equity issue: "They paid their rent here. Why can't they die here?"

Although the house is not intended to be a hospice, Executive Director Tim Budz noted that 80% of residents choose to die there. We believe that these residents' decision to die at BH is related to their emotional attachments and sentiments that equate BH with community, home, and family (see Table 2.2). Jan contrasted institutional death with the feeling that, at BH, one dies among family: "If somebody dies at a nursing home, they won't have a memorial service, balloon service, or all that stuff. When somebody dies, they're gone. You fill that room with somebody else. It's not that way here at BH. It's family."

Even in the face of the mirrors and walls that drive residents away from those who are sick and dying, the desire to comfort and offer support is everpresent. Fellow residents frequently attend to others in the house who are sick or dying—reading to them, bringing them meals, helping with daily chores, and sitting with them and holding their hand during the final moments. Stan said that attending to fellow residents in those moments:

> gives me strength, the help I need to pull through it. I found, even with F., who I wasn't real close to, that right toward the end I was going in as much as I could and reading to him from the Bible, whatever he wanted to hear. He was so frightened because he saw how quickly he went down. He was shoving everybody away. With G., I was there when he died. We had not a half-hour before the last rites.

Having made such visits ourselves, we know these are unsettling, but poignant moments of being both companion and witness.

Offering support during these moments can sometimes be the the most important dialectical test one faces. For in the delicate and precarious participation in the lives of those who are dying, we discover the *paradox of hope*. Herein, the person offering support must balance realism with denial, where practical advice for dying is juxtaposed with hope.

Simon described this paradox when he recalled the situation he faced in advising a very sick resident about obtaining hospice care. Although Simon felt that a hospice would be able to relieve his friend's discomfort and provide 24-hour care, he also recognized that raising this option was like announcing an execution, as the mere mention of a hospice is a marker that one is dying. Pained by this realization, Simon found himself unable to offer the advice that he felt would ultimately provide comfort, but initially dash hope. Simon concluded that, in this case, sustaining hope was more important than palliative care.

Erikson (1976) saw *hope* as the essence of being human, and Karp (1994) elaborated that "even in the most dire circumstances human beings are, remarkably, able to retain hope" (p. 349). Hope not only makes us human, it also serves a therapeutic function. Conner (1994), a pioneer in hospice care, noted that although sustaining hope by those who are dying may appear to be denial, positive illusions (Taylor, 1989) may be therapeutic in avoiding overwhelming anxiety and distress. The professional advice that "you must meet the patient where he or she is," however, can place lay caregivers, in this case fellow residents, in a dialectical tension of denial and realism. From such seeds is born the paradox of hope.

The depression bind, mirrors, walls, and paradox of hope reveal how residents are affected and how they cope with the death and dying that makes social life at BH so precarious. In the following section, we try to capture the insights that emerge from coping with loss.

LOSS AND SELF-REFLECTION

Some poems don't rhyme, and
some stories don't have
a clear beginning,
middle and
end.

—Comedian Gilda Radner, commenting
on her impending death from cancer.

At the time of our second round of interviews, BH had just experienced the loss of over one third of the community due to death or voluntary exits. The trauma of this loss and the revolving-door effect of newcomers were made clear by Anita, a staff member:

[The house] is a little bit more of, kind of islands right now. . . . Probably some of it is we had a very bad January. . . . We lost maybe a third of the community between people moving out and deaths between December and January, so that's 20 people that were left to kind of recoup, and then you introduced another 10 new folks. . . . We have probably five to seven people who have been here a year or more and they're kind of like, "I'm not getting close to anyone else. I just don't want to do this again. This is too tough." So you have that third of the community becoming an island unto themselves or smaller subcommunities and you have the new folks who are always going to be islands, at least in the beginning because they have to get integrated into the group, and then you have a third in-between that's kind of like, "Okay, I don't know which way to go" and tend to group in small subsections until they get some real good sense of what's out there, what else to expect, who to expect it from, and so on.

Sudden or unexpected deaths are not uncommon, but they seem to take a heavier toll on house morale than deaths preceded by a prolonged period of decline. Sudden deaths are harsh reminders of a precarious life, multiple mirrors all at once, of which Mac, although a healthy and active resident at the time of our interview, was acutely aware when he observed, "The human instinct when they go suddenly is, 'Wow, that could happen to me the next day.'" Sudden deaths also deny the opportunity for anticipatory mourning and leave-taking, and can contribute to residents' feeling of "survivor's guilt," that "complex mix of emotions [isolation, loneliness, anxiety, depression, and guilt] seen in those who lived through the Holocaust or who walk away from plane crashes" (Griffin, 1995, p. 5). In talking about a friend and fellow resident who died unexpectedly, Tyler said, "the suddenness of his passing enhanced my survivor's guilt; I keep wondering whether I told him 'I love you' enough."

During the course of our research, we too felt the impact of sudden deaths. We once joked with a robust, lively resident at dinner, who later that evening got an infection, was hospitalized, and died the next day. Along with residents, we experienced the many emotions that accompany unanticipated loss.

In chapter 3, we spoke of the deaths from cancer of the two elderly Alexian Brothers who lived in the house. One of these Brothers, who had retired and needed much-deserved rest, told us he became so bored with retirement that he decided to take the risk to his health and reenter active service as a BH staff member, a choice he said he never regretted. His sudden death was felt deeply; as Glenn, a resident, lamented, "He's not supposed to die."

The social climate at BH during periods of rapid, multiple deaths is described by various residents as being like a morgue, where "a heaviness settles for a day or two" and "life around the place has sort of faded." Josh recounted the dark humor that arises during these heavier moments: "A resident here named B. said she sat down in the dining room while everybody was eating. When she looked up, all she saw were tombstones and everybody behind their tombstones as they were eating. I looked around and saw the same thing she saw . . . so I made a little humor out of it." Later in the interview, Josh provided a searing description of multiple deaths, where, in the cycle of everyday life, his social circle quickly begins to diminish:

When you have several people die in one week, you start to think, "What's happening? We're dying out so quickly." We'll be with each other one day and we're talking, and 3 or 4 days later that person is gone. Ten of us sit in a circle and we talk and have dinner and enjoy each other that day, and we all lay down and go to sleep, and when we wake up there's only nine of us. And we all enjoy each other's company during the day; we sit down and eat and we go through a whole new day of loving each other, and we lay down, sleep, and wake up, and it's only eight. And this process keeps going on and we get up, and it's no more *we* getting up. One person stands up, and they'll have to eat alone, and then they'll have to lay alone, and then they'll have to die alone, and then there's no more.

In spite of the difficulties of living together with a life-threatening illness, coping with the loss of others, and dealing with the constant reminder of one's mortality, some residents see this experience as a preview or lesson for how they, in turn, will be cared for. Alice said, "When I see somebody that's sicker than I am, I just try to do what I can for that individual. I say to myself, 'Someday I might get that way.' I'm not that way now, but someday I might get that way. I would like somebody to look out for me."

The impact of loss is traumatizing, but it also helps residents anticipate and make sense of their own impending deaths. Randy captured this dialectic well:

There have been at least 10 deaths in the house over a 6-month period, so, in one way, it is a very emotional trauma. In another way, it's a very good learning experience. To see the type of support that you have to help you go through that process makes it something less traumatic in my mind. And each individual death is unique and different. Some that have died, I've barely known; some that have died, I've known or come to know, and, consequently, that type of emotional involvement definitely has a profound effect on your emotional stability. The longer I've had the opportunity to think about these things and to experience them, it has really helped me to experience death and dying much better. Had I not been in this environment, I don't think I would have had the opportunity to work through my own stages of death and dying. . . . It has helped prepare me for that aspect of the disease process.

Life at BH is finely tuned to the rapid changes in health and illness among residents. Fear is inevitable, but so, too, is the resilience found in humor, reflection, and in framing loss in ways that become manageable. But at BH, as numerous residents told us, one does not have to do this alone.

THE MYTHOS LEADS THE LOGOS:
MYTH, LANGUAGE, AND BEREAVEMENT RITUALS

Death is never neutral—it challenges our existential being to construct meanings that make sense of life and create a coherent narrative for what appears to be inexplicable. In explaining death, people seek "meaningful, satisfying closures in a slippery world always threatening to open at the seam" (Banks, 1982, p. 24). In a study of *pathographies*—autobiographical and biographical narratives about illness, treatment, and death—Hawkins (1993) identified two central myths: military and journey. These narratives, seen as eternal, permanent truths, provide empowering, integrative, and cohesive meaning structures for these experiences.

The *military myth*, which resonates with the ideology of the medical model, associates disease and illness with warfare:

> We often understand disease as the consequence of a breach in the body's "defense-system": . . . microorganisms invade the body and try to take over while white blood cells quickly come to the body's defense and attack the alien entities; if they conquer them, health is restored. Treatment is similarly militaristic. Common therapies include antibiotics to combat infectious diseases of all sorts, radiation to eradicate enemy cancer cells, and a vast arsenal of chemical weapons . . . employed in the attempt to cure or retard a disease such as cancer or AIDS. (Hawkins, 1993, p. 64)

Alternatively, the *journey myth*, with its quest or pilgrimage motif, evokes the "heroic explanation of the unknown, the dangerous, and the frightening and is thus especially appropriate to experiences of serious illness" (Hawkins, 1993, p. 78). This myth represents "the capacity of the exploring mind, especially the imagination, to transcend a given condition by achieving understanding of and mastery over it" (p. 80).

These myths not only reflect experiences; they can shape the way a person experiences and deals with illness and death, thereby becoming a "model for subsequent *praxis*" (Hawkins, 1993, p. 90). In that regard:

> Such mythic formulations of illness are empowering: the ill person understands the way sickness is like a war or a journey into a distant country; but at the same time he or she is *choosing* to give that meaning to it and this is an act of creative choice in an area of life where choice and creativity are almost wholly denied. (Hawkins, 1993, p. 90)

These myths provide an initial framework for examining the language, worldviews, and the role of ritual in coping with life-threatening illness at BH. However, although the origins of these myths reside in both literary and personal history, these formulations are also shaped by the more immediate social context in which an individual coping with illness is situated, especially in community living.

According to Hawkins (1993), the military myth is more predominant in pathographies about AIDS because it is associated with "power, action and a refusal to be victimized" (p. 88). She also believed that the military myth is more conducive to building community, because the journey myth tends to be "more privatistic, emphasizing the aloneness and isolation" (p. 89).

At BH, however, the military and journey myths comingle; woven together, they help residents and staff make sense of death and build a strong community. For example, staff members embrace the military myth when they speak about their role. Marianne Zelewsky, a member of BH's board of directors, and Linda Venning, a former nurse at BH, believe that "the most important role fulfilled by Bonaventure House's professionals is assisting residents to 'fight the good fight' on their own terms for as long as they live with AIDS" (Zelewsky & Venning, 1993, p. 87). Not surprisingly, "fighting the good fight" has become a central theme in residents' discourse. Sam said, "Last hospitalization the doctors told me, 'You should have been comatose when you got here.' I said, 'I'm too fucking mean to die.' I'm not giving up. Why give up when I know there's people out there with a cure?" Another resident, Peter, said, "I refuse not to keep going . . . I'll be kicking when they take me out of here."

The ideology of fighting AIDS can produce disappointment in those who give up the fight, as Maria explained:

> When I came here, I knew that I was not going to sit down and die because they told me I have AIDS. However, a lot of people that come in here have that misconception. I try to pull them out of it. "You have AIDS, but you don't have to sit down and die." They give up. I don't understand it. I can't lay in a bed and say, "I might as well die, I have AIDS." That doesn't stop you from living.

Pete also expressed frustration with fellow residents who do not fight the disease:

> I see C. and it depresses me, 'cause he's not doing anything for himself. He's not fighting. . . . This is a place to get stabilized, get stronger, not weaker in the mind or body. You get depressed and your body gives up fighting and you're prone to different types of infections. Mentally, you are weak.

In studies of patients with serious chronic illnesses, Engel (1968, 1971) identified a "giving-up, given-up" syndrome, a loss of hope and resolve, that correlates with unexplained sudden death. Clyde gave a gruesome description of fellow residents who had given up:

> Ghoulism. The undead. Their whole life died. They lost their houses, their furniture, their cars, their job. They lost all of that. They died and now they're running around here in their various states of ghoulism. They're dead and there's nothing left. Whereas with me, I gave it all up. I said, "This is a new life for me and I'm starting over." I've adjusted to being here. I'm not a ghoul.

For BH residents, the military myth expressed in the fight against AIDS is tempered by the use of a particular journey myth that emerges from the Christian perspective on health care. Although BH strives toward an ecumenical environment, its religious orientation—grounded in the Catholic tradition—is distinctly Christian. Terms for death, consequently, reflect Christian belief in death as a transition, rather than a final stage of life. Rarely have we heard that a resident "has died"; rather, he or she has "passed away," "passed on," "passed over," or simply "passed." Whereas some may judge this language

as merely euphemistic, the metaphor of "passing" reflects the spiritual orientation of a journey toward an afterlife. This metaphor thus refigures (Ochs, 1993)
the meaning of death by juxtaposing the end of one's life on Earth with the
beginning of a new life with God (see Finnegan, 1995).

The language of passing in this particular journey myth also reflects a more
secular interpretation of a release from suffering. Dying from AIDS is not an
easy death. Even with palliative care, the symptoms and problems of pain
management often result in much physical suffering. As J. L. Martin and Dean
(1993) explained:

> Death due to AIDS is rarely a quiet or peaceful process. [It is] described as an
> emotional roller coaster ... until finally a critical failure due to iatrogenic or natural
> causes leads to death. . . . [T]reatments as well as the illnesses themselves, often
> result in unrelenting nausea, fever, incontinence and wasting. Thus, the lengthy
> time of anticipating death during the later stages of AIDS may be so traumatic that
> any buffering or adaptive function of the anticipatory period may be lost. (p. 321)

However important it is to resist an image of "catastrophic death bed scenes
or one that is transfigured into a sublime spiritual experience" (Kastenbaum,
1994, p. 120), the myriad of chronic and unpredictable debilitating AIDS
symptoms takes a cumulative toll on both PWAs and caregivers. Thus, in both
formal and informal gatherings, residents and staff often talk about death as a
blessing—a release from suffering. John, a resident, said, "As far as death is
concerned, if you're in pain and you're suffering and you've had hardships and
everything like that, deep, deep, deep down inside, your best alternative is to
go. To just let go and go." For the more religious, Christian residents, death is
viewed as a passage to an afterlife, "the great banquet in the sky." As Estella said,
"I feel that the person is in a better position once they've died. They don't have
the disease. I think death is mainly their reward for having gone through so
much hell on earth."

The military and journey myths that characterize the discourse at BH thus
emerge from the take-charge, health-oriented strategy toward the management
of one's illness, coupled with a Christian perspective and pastoral care that view
death as a transition or journey. Together, these myths promote BH's ideology
of "living with AIDS" and, at the same time, encourage residents to transcend
this life and accept the journey that awaits them. Residents are thus offered a
"philosophy [that] heals human diseases ... Its arguments are to the soul as the
doctor's remedies are to the body. They can heal, and they are to be evaluated
in terms of their power to heal" (Nussbaum, 1994, p. 14).

Accompanying these myths and symbols are the collective bereavement
rituals the community uses to cope with loss. Rituals are "organized symbolic
practices and ceremonial activities which serve to define and represent the social
and cultural significance of particular occasions, events or changes" (O'Sullivan,
Hartley, Saunders, Montgomery, & Fiske, 1994, p. 267). Among the most
significant rituals used by all human groups are those that accompany memo-

FIG. 4.2. Memorial services are held in the Brother Joel Troyan, C.F.A. Memorial
Chapel at Bonaventure House. The chapel also serves as a place for quiet meditation,
holiday services, daily mass, Bible study, and other spiritual and/or religious activities
(photograph by Paul Merideth).

rializing and grieving for people who have died (Habenstein & Lamars, 1963).
At BH, bereavement rituals help residents cope with both the loss of fellow
members and the dilemmas posed by the depression bind.

Several personalized rituals assist residents in preparing for their death,
including writing wills, planning their BH memorial service and/or family
funeral, and receiving pastoral counseling. BH offers individual memorial
services in its chapel, depending on the wishes of the deceased (see Fig. 4.2).
Services are usually attended by residents, staff, volunteers, friends, and family.
In addition to the traditional religious format, the BH memorial service gives
those attending a chance to "speak their thoughts" as they remember the
deceased. These expressions are often humorous—foibles, for example, may be
shared—but, for the most part, the person is remembered fondly or idealized.
The tendency to "overidealize and overeulogize the deceased at funerals"
(Worden, 1982, p. 50), however, may inadvertently prolong the grieving process
(see Stroebe & Stroebe, 1987). Perhaps this is why Randy, who told us he was
critical of such rose-colored eulogies, left funds in his will for a private dinner
party for his close friends so that they could say all the things about him that
they couldn't say at his funeral.

There are also unique collective house rituals that are performed when a
resident passes. Residents are notified personally of a death by a staff member
knocking on their doors and sharing the news in private. In the early days of
BH, in the Greco–Roman tradition of publicly announcing that a death had

occurred in a community (see Ochs, 1993), a passing was signaled by a vase in the dining room that had purple silk flowers and said "In memory of _____." However, some residents reacted negatively to this symbol. During an evening meal, Maria looked at the vase and said, "I hate those fucking flowers." The vase was replaced several years ago by burning candles, a traditional Catholic practice, in the foyer and dining room. When residents saw the candles, they knew someone had passed. This practice proved unsettling to at least one resident, who was disturbed by the ambiguity of not knowing who passed. Today, the candle in the dining room is accompanied by a photograph of the deceased. A voluntary emergency support group is also called within 24 hours of someone passing to help residents cope with the loss.

Van Gennep's (1960) seminal work on rites of passage identified transition as the dominant theme of funeral symbolism. The most poignant example of such symbolism at BH, reflecting its unique journey myth, is the balloon ceremony. It started in the early days of BH when a resident requested that balloons be released outside as part of his memorial service. At this ceremony people receive colored balloons tied to long ribbons; remembrances of the deceased are spoken, and then the balloons are released simultaneously. The sight of the balloons flying up in unison typically evokes cathartic laughter and the joy so commonly associated with their everyday release (see Fig. 4.3).

The Executive Director explained how this ceremony became a common BH ritual:

> The idea caught on quickly, and many residents after [the first time] asked for the balloon ceremony to happen. It sort of emerged as a house tradition now, where even if a person doesn't ask for that as part of his or her personal funeral plan, it is something the house does on a regular basis to memorialize people who have passed.

The balloon ceremony ritual is a compelling example of *symbolic reversal* (Cohen, 1985), a process used by disenfranchised groups to redefine the negative connotations of symbols by inverting them so as to promote positive feelings and self-image (e.g., the inversion represented by the slogan "Black is beautiful"). In the balloon ceremony, the letting go of the balloons symbolically reverses a sad occasion of mourning into a celebration of relief and release.

We are struck by the contrast between traditional bereavement services, such as funerals, and the balloon ceremony at BH. Although both are designed to provide a sense of closure and release for mourners, they appear to do so in dramatically different ways. At grave-site funerals, the dress code is black, the bereaved view the closed casket, and reverently look down as it is lowered into the ground. The funeral is usually carefully choreographed by a religious or spiritual leader. The atmosphere is often strained and very solemn, and a quietness prevails as those attending become silent onlookers and then drift off in isolated clusters.

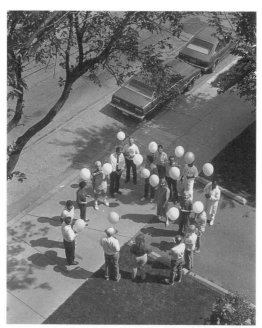

FIG. 4.3.   The balloon ceremony, occurring within a week after a resident has passed, is a poignant example of funeral symbolism. The sight of the balloons flying up in unison typically evokes the cathartic laughter and joy so commonly associated with their every-day release, turning a sad occasion into a celebration of relief and release from the pain of living with AIDS (photograph by Paul Merideth).

FIG. 4.3. The balloon ceremony (cont.).

In sharp contrast, the spirit, emotions, and physical experience of the BH balloon ceremony are uplifting. Although we have attended some balloon ceremonies that felt almost perfunctory, most of these ceremonies are exhilarating. They demonstrate what Durkheim (1965) called "collective effervescence," an aspect of sociability where the individual experiences "belonging to a whole greater than the sum of its parts, of being carried away by a group 'spirit'" (Csikszentmihalyi & Rochberg-Halton, 1981, p. 34). The symbolic value of this reversal and the spirit of this ceremony were commented on by Alec, a staff member:

> When we are outside doing the balloon ceremony and a balloon gets stuck, we talk about the person not actually being ready to go. People make jokes, but it's real. People feel a connection to that, that something's undone. It [the balloon] will be gone sometimes, but sometimes they hang around for a really long time, and other times it's gone within seconds. That's a real allegory for a lot of people.

Randy, a resident, captured the symbolism and almost celebratory nature of this bereavement ritual most vividly: "It's a letting go of someone who is unique and special. I think the symbolism is very important to the whole process, from birth to death—that we celebrate life and we end life with a celebration."

Another collective practice that has become an annual bereavement ritual is the BH quilt donated to the AIDS Memorial Quilt, sponsored by The NAMES Project Foundation. This project collects the names of those who died from AIDS on individual 3-by-6 foot memorial panels, the size of a human grave, and publicly shows them in this visually moving way to illustrate the enormity of the AIDS epidemic, and as a creative means for remembrance and healing. Clive Jones, creator of the AIDS Memorial Quilt, chose this form because of the connotations of warmth and humanity associated with quilts (see Ruskin, 1988), and there is a rich history to commemorative mourning quilts (see Trechsel, 1990). Quilts have also been used traditionally by women as a political expression of their marginality (e.g., to advocate abolition, suffrage, and temperance; see Finnegan, 1995). Thus, "the appropriation of an historically undervalued form of discourse, quilting, performed by an historically undervalued group, women, links gay men and persons-with-AIDS to a history of using quilting as a way to gain 'voice'" (Finnegan, 1995, p. 9).

The AIDS Memorial Quilt has become the largest ongoing community art project in the world, with more than 40 NAMES Project chapters in the United States and 32 independent Quilt initiatives from around the world (The NAMES Project Foundation, 1996a). As a site of participatory ritual (Strine, Long, & Hopkins, 1990) that invites friends, lovers, and family members to sew together, and observers to mourn together, the Quilt helps create and sustain community. Clive Jones said, "I never imagined that the simple act of sewing quilts would bind together people of very different backgrounds" (The NAMES Project Foundation, 1996b).

The sense of community created by the AIDS Memorial Quilt is readily apparent at BH, where residents, staff, and volunteers congregate night after night in the dining room for a sewing bee (see Fig. 4.4). The 1995 BH quilt incorporated 63 colorful balloons to memoralize each resident who died between 1993–1995. Thus, the balloon symbology from the memorial ceremony is adapted to another medium. As Frey, Adelman, and Query (1996) noted, "The balloon image in this tangible, lasting memorial demonstrates the power of this metaphor for bereavement (e.g., symbolizing the process of 'letting go') and for representing the journey myth of death-as-transition" (p. 393).

As a result of AIDS activist movements and the gay communities, balloon ceremonies and memorial quilts have emerged as innovative and emotionally healing rituals for bereavement. This is readily visible in television programs and films and at large-scale events, such as the unfolding of the AIDS Memorial Quilt on America's front lawn, the National Mall in Washington, DC, where the October 11–13, 1996 presentation is expected to include 45,000 panels and cover more than 27 acres or about 29 football fields (The NAMES Project Foundation, 1995). Several BH residents flew at their own expense to the last unfolding of the Quilt in DC, and some are currently making plans to attend the 1996 presentation, because the Quilt will include 86 names of BH residents (Scott M. Williams, Communications Coordinator, The NAMES Project Foundation, personal communication, June 13, 1996). For BH residents, their

FIG. 4.4. Making a Bonaventure House quilt for the AIDS Memorial Quilt, sponsored by the NAMES Project Foundation, has become an annual bereavement ritual that bonds together residents, staff, and volunteers in their desire to memorialize BH residents who have passed. Sewers choose someone they wish to memorialize and make a small quilt for him or her. These small quilts are then assembled into a larger quilt that travels across the country with the AIDS Memorial Quilt
(photograph by Paul Merideth).

most intense and private moments of grief are now mediated by membership in a much larger community, thus allowing them to transcend the concrete walls of the house and the sorrow contained within.

Rituals are typically acknowledged for their symbolic value in creating a shared world among group members. They "both express and reinforce jointly-held values and represent ways of coming together as a group, of feeling closer to one another. For this reason, rituals are often the most significant and important aspect of community life to members" (Kanter, 1972, p. 47). At BH, bereavement rituals capture the essence of the particular journey myth that is echoed in the religious memorial service, the secular balloon ceremony, and the collaborative memorial quilt.

The power of these rituals, however, goes beyond symbolic value, for ritual is one of the most important communicative forms for managing dialectical tensions (see Altman, Brown, Staples, & Werner, 1992; Bell, 1992; Bochner, 1984; Philipsen, 1987; Turner, 1969; Werner & Baxter, 1994). As Roberts (1988) observed, "Ritual can hold both sides of a contradiction at the same time. We all live with the ultimate paradoxes of life/death, connection/distance, ideal/real, good/evil. Ritual can incorporate both sides of contradictions so that they can be managed simultaneously" (p. 16). By helping residents to bracket mourning and grieve efficiently, thereby avoiding further depression of their immune system, these rituals serve a critical psychosocial function in helping residents manage the dialectical tensions of the depression bind.

These rituals, moreover, play a crucial role in reintegrating residents into BH community life. Littlewood (1992) noted that ritually bracketing the time for mourning "acts as an important aid to the bereaved person's re-entry into social life" (p. 30). By articulating contexts and parameters for grieving, these social practices play a central role in both defining loss and keeping individuals from getting mired in grief (Rosenblatt, 1993). These rituals are thus critical to the reintegration and functioning of the collective; for however great the loss, residents must still meet the exigencies of daily life, house maintenance, and the reality of a new day.

Lest we fall into the trap of overestimating the transformative power of myths and rituals, we are reminded of Parkes' (1993) caution that "grief is not a unitary phenomenon" (p. 92), and neither is its resolution. Indeed, death itself is not a singular, predictable experience. Hawkins (1993) observed that, although we have a plethora of *ars moriendi*, viable models for how to die, there is a:

> frantic and uncritical way in which we seem to be creating individual versions of how to die. Perhaps one reason why the work of dying seems so difficult today is that the individual is expected not only to face his or her death—in itself a task arduous enough—but also to create a way of dying out of the fragments of ideologies and religious sentiments that our culture provides us. (p. 124)

Prescriptions for "good patient behavior" and "dignified death" do little to empower or comfort. As Zook (1994) contended, the meaningful experience of "health for the terminally ill, however paradoxically sounding, may be attained through orienting toward death in an authentic, meaningful manner. . . . Even in death, the pursuit of authenticity promotes resistance to attempts to 'normalize' or 'script' experience" (p. 364).

Bonaventure House walks a fine line in this regard. The ideology and practices of living with AIDS and the Christian perspective of a journey to the afterlife are dominant paradigms meant to help residents get ready for death and cope with the loss of others in particular ways. In part, this hegemony is softened by diverse, voluntary services offered to residents for constructing their own reality for coping, even when this involves alternative religious practices, such as daily Buddhist chantings or even voodooism. But if residents so choose, the dominant ideology and practices offered at BH can provide a source of great comfort, a coherent narrative for the chaos that threatens both the individual and the collective.

In our experience at BH, the diverse and more private expressions of bereavement and dying with AIDS were found in the silent symbolism of personal possessions that are displayed or exchanged informally. We expand on these communicative practices in the following section to provide a glimpse into personalized—yet collective—forms of coping with loss and impending death.

SPIRITS IN THE MATERIAL WORLD: BEREAVEMENT AND POSSESSIONS

> The past is hidden . . .
> beyond the reach of the intellect—
> in some material object.
>
> —Marcel Proust

We were standing outside BH one day, talking with Maria, one of the residents. On seeing the new buds from flowers planted by a resident who had died several years ago, she told us that these flowers bloom annually. "You see," she said, "he's telling us he's still around." Reminders—the painting by M. in the foyer, the sculpture with a picture of his lover donated by R. on the 3rd floor, the antique theatre posters from C.'s collection in the hallway, and the blooming flowers from D. outside—speak of how possessions serve as visible legacies.

A central theme in prior work on dispossession—the letting go of possessions—is the role that objects play in facilitating and reflecting identity transformation during various life passages (see McAlexander, 1991; McAlexander, Schouten, & Roberts, 1993; M. M. Young, 1991). In the context of BH, prior to and after death, possessions serve two major functions: the artifacts are symbols by which individuals wish to be remembered, and they become vehicles of social communication (Olson, 1985) for expressing communion and parting. As Adelman (1992) contended, "The symbolic meaning of the object itself and its use in facilitating interaction can serve as rituals for departing, as spiritual companions for those who survive, and as visible markers for reaffirming community purpose" (p. 401).

The material world is a symbolic extension of the self (Belk, 1988); dispossession thus symbolizes a disassembling of the self. Wills, for example, serve as legal and symbolic expressions of both detachment from prized material goods and relational attachment to those to whom the goods are bequeathed. At BH, dispossession is more informal, typically taking the form of gift giving. One resident, a Native American who was an avid thrift-store shopper, began leaving things at fellow residents' doors in an unspoken gesture of leave-taking. Maria, a close friend of his, noted, "I'd get up in the morning and discover something hanging on my door and, sure enough, I knew it was him. We all knew it was him. Even after he was gone, when things would disappear or reappear [after being momentarily lost], we would say, 'Oh, it's just him.'"

Sometimes a gift is given not to any particular resident, but to the BH community. Randy, for example, made his own documentary film about BH (and asked Mara for assistance) to help newcomers during the orientation process that would serve as his legacy to the house.

Possessions become part of the collective memory, incorporating the deceased into the community culture. They trigger stories and are tangible legacies of incidents and the personalities of those who have passed. This phenomenon is what Myeroff (1982) referred to as *re-membering*—an act of recollection that promotes "purposive, significant unification, quite different from the passive, continuous fragmentary flickering of images and feelings that accompany other activities in the normal flow of consciousness" (p. 111).

In her review and critique of memory studies, Zelizer (1995) noted:

> [C]ollective memory often resides in the artifacts that mark its existence. Cultural forms, such as monuments, diaries, fashion trends, television retrospectives, museum openings, and fashion shows, all house memories in a durable fashion, anchoring the transient and variable nature of memory itself. This makes the materiality of memory user-friendly. It also makes cultural forms a necessary part of memory's analysis. (p. 232)

Collective memory resides not only in mass media and large-scale artifacts; for smaller groups, collective remembering is housed in more localized forms. One of the most striking collections of bequeathed artifacts at BH is found in one resident's room, which she refers to as the "Museum of Memories" (see Fig. 4.5). After entering BH with just two bags of clothes, her room was filled with the possessions of others long passed—photos, key chains, and memorabilia line the walls. Because she is a close friend of ours, she sometimes invited us to her room, and it was not uncommon to find our memories triggered by some object and then to spend time recalling a resident who had passed, or a special occasion that occurred at BH.

Within both private rooms and public spaces, the most cherished and popular gifts are photographs that are displayed openly or kept in personal and community scrapbooks. Csikszentmihalyi and Rochberg-Halton (1981) noted that in most cultures around the world, "[T]he memory of ancestors is preserved in one form or another. . . . [In the past] a house was not a home without a shrine where each departed person was represented by a symbol of his or her former existence . . . . In our times photos seem to fulfill this function" (p. 69). Like the AIDS Memorial Quilt, the construction and sharing of a resident's scrapbook has become not only a ritualized memorial to times past, but also a tribute to a lifestyle and to friendships now devastated by AIDS.

Besides the private scrapbooks kept by individual residents, there are nine full scrapbooks of house photographs that recount the history of BH. These books are worn and smudged by frequent use and have become like reference books that document and verify people, events, and periods of the house. The photographs are mostly images of festive occasions, such as parties, social outings, special meals, and important visitors (e.g., the mayor of Chicago). There are also specialized albums, such as thematic portrayals of special events

FIG. 4.5. This resident entered Bonaventure House with only two bags of clothes. Two years later, her room is filled with gifts and photographs given to her from many residents who have passed. She refers to her room as the "Museum of Memories" (photograph by Paul Merideth).

(like the summer retreat at a country cabin), collections of portraits of residents who have passed, or humorous parodies of the staff.

We often see residents pore over these scrapbooks, like students with a history book. For insiders, "going over the scrapbook together serves as a kind of intensification ritual, re-validating interpersonal bonds, and mutually enriching participants' perspectives on past events" (Katriel & Farrell, 1991, p. 12). A resident once pulled out a scrapbook to help us remember a resident who had passed, at the same time that another resident was enthusiastically showing us pictures from the house during the previous summer. In this way, BH scrapbooks provide an important link between individuals and the collective; they help to "refigure the world into a place of belonging, a *home*" (Katriel & Farrell, 1991, p. 15).

An extension of these traditional scrapbooks can be seen in one of the stairwells at BH, where there are portraits of residents taken by Paul Merideth, the house photographer. Maria, a resident, named this stairwell "The Hall of Fame" (see Fig. 4.6).

Merideth, whose photographs of BH have appeared in newspapers and public exhibits (1992a, 1992b, 1992c), and are reprinted throughout this book, uses this medium to pay tribute to the people of BH. An example is his tribute to Robert Thomas (see Fig. 4.7), with whom he established a close relationship over an 8-month period. His visual photographic narratives provide unique and creative perspectives on interpreting the BH experience.

In most cases, the photographs bequeathed to others are what we refer to as *well images*, pictures of residents when they are physically healthy. For example, after a long and intensely close relationship between a resident named Randy and Mara, at their last meeting he gave her an 8 x 12, matte-finished photograph of himself taken when he was still visibly healthy. Throughout the 6 years of visiting residents' rooms, the only self-portraits we see displayed are well images (see the well image on the wall in Fig. 4.8). Given the physical devastation (particularly facial disfigurement) accompanying AIDS symptoms, these well images are forms of self-preservation, healthy images of themselves that residents desire to remember and affirm. When given as gifts, these photographs represent the way residents wish others to visually memorialize and remember them.

Well images stand in sharp contrast to the way people with AIDS are typically portrayed in photographs. As Sokolowski (cited in Crimp, 1992) contended in his discussion of photographer Rosalind Solomon's exhibition, entitled *Portraits in the Time of AIDS*, "Popular representations of AIDS have been devoid of depictions of people living with AIDS, save for the lurid journalistic images of patients *in extremis*, published in the popular press where the subjects are depicted as decidedly *not* persons *living* with AIDS, but as victims" (p. 120). PWAs usually are shown as "ravaged, disfigured, and debilitated by the syndrome; they are generally alone, desperate, but resigned to their 'inevitable' deaths" (Crimp, 1992, p. 118). The popular before-and-after AIDS pictures reinforce "the before-and-after conventions of traditional medical photography

FIG. 4.6.   The "Hall of Fame," as residents call this stairwell on the third floor of
Bonaventure House, is lined with photographs of house residents,
many of whom have passed (photograph by Paul Merideth).

with the before–after conventions of standard photojournalistic practice. An emphasis is all but invariably placed on the question of fatality" (Watny, 1994, p. 65).

We take this critique seriously and debated whether to include Merideth's tribute to Robert Thomas. Our decision was based on our observations of Paul's respectful and unobtrusive sensitivity when he works with residents, and his close collaboration and friendship with Robert over the 8-month project. Paul volunteers his services free of charge to BH, and residents are proud that his work graces the halls, stairwells, and the private rooms of the house. We feel his work is not a crass pastiche, but a sensitive and deeply felt portrayal of Robert.

Popular visual portrayals thus too often unfairly represent people with AIDS as physically disgusting, socially questionable, and morally repugnant. It is not surprising, therefore, that such groups as ACT UP demand that PWAs be shown as "vibrant, loving, sexy, beautiful, acting up and fighting back" (Crimp, 1992, p. 118). The most prevalent photographs at BH clearly are of this type. However, displacing negative images solely with positive ones, Crimp argued,

FIG. 4.7. Eight Months With Robert Thomas; Paul Merideth's tribute to Robert Thomas. Paul Merideth, the house photographer, documents the lives of residents and BH social life. He befriended and worked with Robert Thomas, a much-loved resident at BH, to cocreate this photographic essay of Robert's last 8 months.

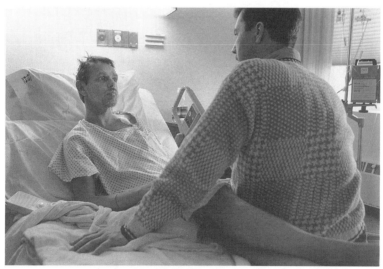

FIG. 4.7. (cont.)   When I first met Robert in August 1990, he was still relatively healthy and strong. He was 41. He had 8 months left. Robert, who had made a good living selling financial affairs, arranged a living will, and purchased a vault for himself at Rosehill Cemetery. He labeled the drawers of his dresser so that when he became too weak to care for himself, the volunteers would know not to put his socks in his underwear drawer. As his condition worsened, he seemed to relish smaller and smaller things; a poem read to him by a friend; the smell of the air in spring, his last.

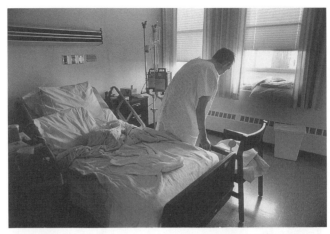

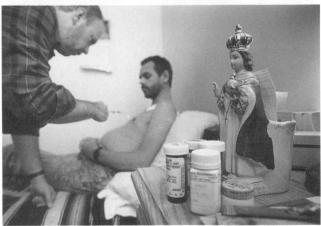

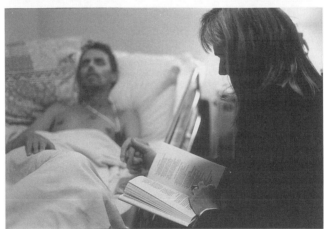

FIG. 4.7. (cont.)   For some residents, Bonaventure House is their only home, and its community their only family. Robert was one of these.

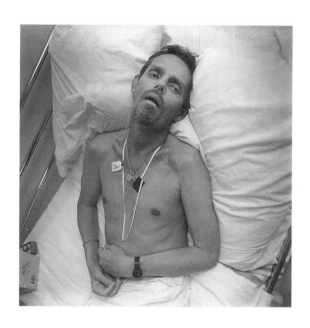

FIG. 4.7. (cont.)   His closest living relative, a sister somewhere in the south whom he loved very much, never came to visit him. She has two kids. She was afraid. He never complained. She sent a beautiful bouquet of flowers when he died.

—Paul Merideth

is but another way of treating a person as an "other." The difficulty of capturing both images is illustrated in Fig. 4.8; by including a positive image with the more typical sick image, the photograph cannot escape its own bind of becoming a before-and-after image. Cognizant of this dilemma, we tried to select photographs that portray with dignity the ways people with AIDS lead their lives.

Dispossession and acquisition of residents' goods, scrapbooks, and personal portraits serve as material legacies that symbolically assemble and disassemble social relationships. They are also silent testimony that although residents may have died from AIDS, they *lived* at BH.

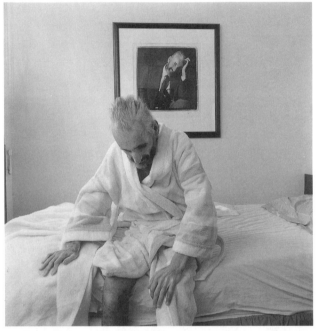

FIG. 4.8.   Sitting in front of his favorite self-portrait, a well image, in his private room, this resident passed shortly after this photograph was taken (photograph by Paul Merideth).

✽ ✽ ✽ ✽ ✽ ✽ ✽ ✽ ✽ ✽

Myths, language, rituals, and gifts demonstrate the grand and small gestures that comprise collective practices for coping with loss at Bonaventure House. Residents know they will neither die alone nor be forgotten. Though the pulse of everyday life is made fragile by loss, for those who live on, the reality that the community never stops provides an imperative for collective recovery. For the next day, "the trains run on time": the house meeting convenes at 10, lunch is served at noon, and, yes, that "damn" dish duty awaits as usual.

Epilogue: Stability Amidst the Fragility

The concept of community offers a compelling model of connection that has caught the imagination of scholars and the public alike: "The intellectual engagement with community bursts across boundaries with abandon" (Fowler, 1991, p. 2). But however it is defined, community is not a disembodied concept; it is always enacted by "concrete human beings acting in specific contexts" (Fuoss, 1995, p. 81), and best studied in particular settings like Bonaventure House.

Bonaventure House is a poignant drama—tenuous, marginal, and insulated—a distilled experience of social life created and sustained in crisis. Few crises are more profound than death, especially so when the loss is due to AIDS. However, rather than a black hole—an unsettling reflection—Bonaventure House can be a lesson. For amidst the fragility, we conclude that stability is created and sustained through three critical features: accepting and respecting dialectical tensions; enacting communicative practices that encourage the expression of conflicting points of view; and seeing community as a never-ending process embedded in both mundane and grand gestures. Furthermore, we believe that these features can extend to strengthening the precarious connections within our enduring environments.

A dialectical perspective embraces the complexity of community life by accepting and respecting the multiplicity of voices that reflect different experiences, expectations, needs, and goals. Community is an "essentially contested concept" (Gallie, 1964, p. 158). There is no single, dominant, romantic ideal; rather, a variety of oppositional views must be accommodated. "Community and contestation are not oppositional forces but flip sides of the same social process as indivisible from one another as the front and back sides of a sheet of paper" (Fuoss, 1995, p. 94).

The acceptance of a dialectical perspective at Bonaventure House is well-illustrated by the complex relationship between the individual residents and the collective. The creation of community at Bonaventure House does not come from privileging the collective at the expense of the individual—a common fear in the United States. Granted, the leaders of Bonaventure House do seek a collective conception of the house as more than a hotel or a hospice, more than a disembodied shelter or a frantic final stop. They envision a place that fosters collective healing, solace, and compassion. But at the same time, they are willing to experiment and be open to the needs of individual residents, although residents' preferences are not always fulfilled. Throughout the years, administrators, staff members, residents, and volunteers consistently make choices to strengthen the collective while simultaneously trying to respect the individual members—no easy task. As Bonaventure House reveals, the line between individual and collective well-being is tenuous, generating a "dialectic in which each is a condition for the other" (I. M. Young, 1995, p. 240).

At the heart of Bonaventure House's community are communicative practices that encourage the expression of conflicting points of views. As Smith and Berg (1987) maintained:

> The simultaneous expression of these contradictory reactions actually makes the group a safe place, albeit a place full of opposing forces. . . . Emotionally, a group that does not provide room for the conflicting and ambivalent reactions evoked by group life is not a place where either the individuals or the group as a whole can thrive. (pp. 16, 83)

The diverse communicative practices and feedback systems at Bonaventure House help make it a safe place where people feel comfortable expressing their differences and conflicts. To use a mixed metaphor, the very safety of these practices is in the fault lines on which individual, relational, and collective rights are tested and confirmed.

These communicative practices help create what Friedman (1986) called a "community of otherness," as opposed to a "community of affinity" or likemindedness that is "always false community . . . made up of people who huddle together for security . . . because they are so afraid of conflict and opposition" (p. xv). In contrast, "conflict is not feared in a 'community of otherness.' . . . [It] permits a struggle over ideas and principles, while confirming one's adversary, . . . encouraging confirmation of persons, even when their ideas clash with those of the majority" (Arnett, 1986, p. 8).

Communication is the primary social process, as Pearce (1989) claimed, that creates space for multiple and oppositional voices to be heard, and through which self, other, and the collective are created and sustained. As Barber (1984) argued, "At the heart of a strong democracy is talk" (p. 173). Bonaventure House reveals that community is a particular type of conversation, grounded in *dialogue*, not monologue. Theologian Thomas Merton (1961) expressed the point eloquently: "Mere living alone does not isolate a man, mere living together does not bring men into communion. To live in communion, in genuine dialogue with others, is absolutely necessary if man is to remain human" (p. 55).

To achieve communion and, therefore, community, people must find common symbols and collective practices that help them cope with the tensions of group and organizational life. As Conquergood (1992) argued, "People need concrete symbols through which they can grasp elusive meanings and discharge deep and contradictory feelings" (p. 107). Sharing significant symbols "help communities impose order on experiences which are often chaotic" (Proctor, 1990, p. 118). Bonaventure House has a rich array of shared symbols that helps create order out of the chaos of coping with constant loss and impending death, from the concrete burning candles that signal passing to the more mythic constructions for fighting the disease and then letting go.

Bonaventure House thus shows how community is created and sustained in symbolic practices. It further reveals that any collective practice is potentially both a blessing and a curse, simultaneously exacerbating and diminishing the tensions of daily life. These tensions are not necessarily resolved, but they can be massaged through communicative practices.

Walking this dialectical tightrope occurs day by day, encounter by encounter. Formulaic approaches to community construction in the form of handbooks, rulebooks, and development plans defy the organic, incomplete, and evolving nature of this process. A college administrator once asked us, the authors, how Bonaventure House might prove useful to his constituents, and we responded that efforts to cultivate community are rarely pristine, orderly, or even predictable. Just as children (and some adults) often drop their possessions in a disorderly fashion to signal their rebelliousness and sense of place, community also entails a sense of ownership that is often messy. It should not be treated like a "construction project, something to be achieved by a certain date, as if community could ever be finished" (Fowler, 1995, p. 95), for it is an "emergent process ... continually in flux" (Proctor, 1990, p. 130). The metaphor of journey invoked so pervasively in the discourse at Bonaventure House captures well the processual nature of community, for "people living together with AIDS are pilgrims embarking on a frightening journey" (Adelman & Frey, 1994, p. 21), with almost no maps to guide them. In the words of Tony, a staff member at Bonaventure House, "Believe it or not, folks, we are writing the book."

Perhaps most important, community is best expressed in "ordinary motives, spontaneous gestures and everyday actions" (R. C. Solomon, 1989, p. 355). Grand ceremonies at Bonaventure House in the form of bereavement rituals and collective celebrations accentuate group spirit. But that spirit is embedded and woven more tightly in everyday, even mundane, gestures: bringing a food tray to someone who is sick, giving a person a ride to the airport, or offering the hug someone needs. As well, it is the gripes, gossip, and fights that challenge people and, in the process, bind them more firmly together.

By focusing on concrete and everyday gestures, Bonaventure House rejects the elevation of community to the unattainable quest for the "Holy Grail" that precludes its achievement. R. C. Solomon's (1989) warning about social justice applies equally well to community, where the grand, heroic, and even divine conception often "awes rather than motivates us" (p. 355). As a result of these bigger-than-life constructions, we place it, like social justice, "at a distance, something other, a state to be hoped for or prayed for but just for that reason something probably unlikely, even impossible, perhaps even a delusion. . . . [It] is out of our hands, a matter of personal concern but not a matter of individual responsibility" (R. C. Solomon, 1989, p. 355).

All too often in the course of everyday life—at work, school, and even in our homes—opportunities for enhancing the quality of community life elude us. Bonaventure House shows that we are always making choices about the social worlds we can potentially create; that we need to be bolder in taking risks that foster diversity, discarding old routines, and experimenting with new ones. Maybe we should take our cue from the people of Bonaventure House when they altered their traditional weekly meeting, and *not* conduct "business as usual." For here, amidst the chaos that characterizes this fragile experience, a group of strangers comes together to create and sustain community—surely, this is a lesson for us all.

❊ ❊ ❊ ❊ ❊ ❊ ❊ ❊ ❊ ❊

Most of the residents you read about have passed.
We hope we served their voices well.

References

Abdel-Hamlin, A. A. (1982). Social support and managerial affective responses to job stress. *Journal of Occupational Behavior, 3,* 281–295.

Adelman, M. B. (1989). Social support and AIDS. *AIDS & Public Policy Journal, 4,* 31–39.

Adelman, M. B. (1992). Rituals of adversity and remembering: The role of possessions for persons and community living with AIDS. In J. F. Sherry, Jr. & B. Sternthal (Eds.), *Advances in consumer research* (Vol. 19, pp. 201–403). Provo, UT: Association for Consumer Research.

Adelman, M. B., & Frey, L. R. (1994). The pilgrim must embark: Creating and sustaining community in a residential facility for people with AIDS. In L. R. Frey (Ed.), *Group communication in context: Studies of natural groups* (pp. 3–21). Hillsdale, NJ: Lawrence Erlbaum Associates.

Adelman, M. B., Frey, L. R., & Budz, T. (1994). Keeping the community spirit alive. *Journal of Long-Term Care Administration, 22*(2), 4–7.

Adelman, M. B. (Producer), & Schultz, P. (Director). (1991). *The pilgrim must embark: Living in community* [Videotape]. Chicago: Terra Nova Films.

Albert, E. (1986). Acquired Immune Deficiency Syndrome: The victim and the press. *Studies in Communication, 3,* 135–158.

Albert, S., & Whetten, D. (1985). Organizational identity. In L. L. Cummings & B. M. Staw (Eds.), *Research in organizational behavior* (Vol. 7, pp. 263–295). Greenwich, CT: JAI.

Albrecht, T. L., & Adelman, M. B. (1987a). Communicating social support: A theoretical perspective. In T. L. Albrecht, M. B. Adelman, & Associates, *Communicating social support* (pp. 18–39). Newbury Park, CA: Sage.

Albrecht, T. L., & Adelman, M. B. (1987b). Dilemmas of supportive communication. In T. L. Albrecht, M. B. Adelman, & Associates, *Communicating social support* (pp. 240–254). Newbury Park, CA: Sage.

Albrecht, T. L., Burleson, B. R., & Goldsmith, D. (1994). Supportive communication. In M. L. Knapp & G. R. Miller (Eds.), *Handbook of interpersonal communication* (2nd ed., pp. 419–449). Thousand Oaks, CA: Sage.

Allen, B. J. (1995). "Diversity" and organizational communication. *Journal of Applied Communication Research, 23,* 143–155.

Altman, I. (1993). Dialectics, physical environments, and personal relationships. *Communication Monographs, 60,* 26–34.

Altman, I., Brown, B. B., Staples, B., & Werner, C. M. (1992). A transactional approach to close relationships: Courtship, weddings and placemaking. In B. Walsh, K. Craik, & R. Price (Eds.), *Person-environment psychology* (pp. 193–241). Hillsdale, NJ: Lawrence Erlbaum Associates.

Altman, I., & Low, S. M. (Eds.). (1992). *Place attachment. Human behavior and environment: Advances in theory and research* (Vol. 12). New York: Plenum.

Altman, I., Vinsel, A., & Brown, B. B. (1981). Dialectical conceptions in social psychology: An application to social penetration and privacy regulation. In L. Berkowitz (Ed.), *Advances in experimental social psychology* (Vol. 14, pp. 257–273). New York: Wiley.

Argyle, M., Furnham, A., & Graham, J. (1981). *Social situations.* Cambridge, MA: Cambridge University Press.

Argyris, C., & Schon, D. (1978). *Organizational learning: A theory of action perspective*. Reading, MA: Addison-Wesley.

Arnett, R. C. (1986). *Communication and community: Implications of Martin Buber's dialogue*. Carbondale: Southern Illinois University Press.

Ashford, S. (1986). Feedback-seeking in individual adaptation: A resource perspective. *Academy of Management Journal, 29*, 465–487.

Ashford, S., & Cummings, L. (1985). Proactive feedback seeking: The instrumental use of the information environment. *Journal of Occupational Psychology, 58*, 67–79.

Askham, J. (1976). Identity and stability within the marriage relationship. *Journal of Marriage and the Family, 38*, 535–547.

Bakhtin, M. M. (1968). *Rabelais and his world* (H. Iswolsky, Trans.). Bloomington: Indiana University Press. (Original work published 1965)

Bakhtin, M. M. (1984). *Problems of Dostoevsky's poetics* (C. Emerson, Ed. & Trans.). Minneapolis: University of Minnesota Press. (Original work published 1929)

Banks, S. A. (1982). Once upon a time: Interpretation in literature and medicine. *Literature and Medicine, 1*, 23–27.

Barber, B. (1984). *Strong democracy: Participatory politics for a new age*. Berkeley: University of California Press.

Barker, J. R., & Cheney, G. (1994). The concept and the practices of discipline in contemporary organizational life. *Communication Monographs, 61*, 19–43.

Barnlund, D. C. (1988). Communication in a global village. In L. A. Samovar & R. E. Porter (Eds.), *Intercultural communication: A reader* (5th ed., pp. 5–14). Belmont, CA: Wadsworth.

Bateson, M. C., & Goldsby, R. (1988). *Thinking AIDS: The social response to the biological threat*. Reading, MA: Addison-Wesley.

Baxter, L. A. (1988). A dialectical perspective on communication strategies in relationship development. In S. Duck (Ed.), *Handbook of personal relationships: Theory, research, and interventions* (pp. 257–273). New York: Wiley.

Baxter, L. A. (1990). Dialectical contradictions in relationship development. *Journal of Social and Personal Relationships, 7*, 69–88.

Baxter, L. A., & Montgomery, B. M. (1996). *Relating: Dialogues and dialectics*. New York: Guilford.

Baxter, L. A., & Simon, E. P. (1993). Relationship maintenance strategies and dialectical contradictions in personal relationships. *Journal of Social and Personal Relationships, 10*, 225–292.

Belk, R. W. (1988). Possessions and the extended self. *Journal of Consumer Research, 15*, 139–168.

Bell, C. (1992). *Ritual theory, ritual practice*. New York: Oxford University Press.

Bellah, R. N., Madsen, R., Sullivan, W. M., Swidler, A., & Tipton, S. M. (1985). *Habits of the heart: Individualism and commitment in American life*. New York: Harper & Row.

Bellah, R. N., Madsen, R., Sullivan, W. M., Swidler, A., & Tipton, S. M. (1991). *The good society*. New York: Knopf.

Berg, P. (1985). Organization change as a symbolic transformation process. In P. J. Frost, L. F. Moore, M. R. Louis, G. C. Lundberg, & J. Martin (Eds.), *Organizational culture* (pp. 281–299). Beverly Hills, CA: Sage.

Bettendorf, F. (1993). In the Alexian spirit. In S. J. Miller, K. I. Ward, & R. Rybicki (Eds.), *Handbook for assisted living* (pp. 5–6). Chicago: Bonaventure House.

Bochner, A. (1984). The functions of human communication in interpersonal bonding. In C. Arnold & J. W. Bowers (Eds.), *Handbook of rhetorical and communication theory* (pp. 544–621). Boston: Allyn & Bacon.

Bormann, E. G. (1983). Symbolic convergence: Organizational communication and culture. In L. Putnam & M. E. Pacanowsky (Eds.), *Communication and organizations: An interpretive approach* (pp. 99–122). Beverly Hills, CA: Sage.

Bormann, E. G. (1986). Symbolic convergence theory and communication in group decision-making. In R. Y. Hirokawa & M. S. Poole (Eds.), *Communication and group decision-making* (pp. 219–236). Beverly Hills, CA: Sage.

Bormann, E. G. (1996). Symbolic convergence theory and communication in group decision-making. In R. Y. Hirokawa & M. S. Poole (Eds.), *Communication and group decision-making* (2nd ed., pp. 81–113). Thousand Oaks, CA: Sage.

Boyer, E. P., & Webb, T. G. (1992). Ethics and diversity: A correlation enhanced through corporate communication. *IEEE Transactions on Professional Communication, 35,* 38–43.

Boyle, L. (1993). Alcohol and other drug abuse recovery. In S. J. Miller, K. I. Ward, & R. Rybicki (Eds.), *Handbook for assisted living* (pp. 91–98). Chicago: Bonaventure House.

Brandt, A. M. (1985). *No magic bullet: A social history of venereal disease in the United States since 1880.* New York: Oxford University Press.

Bridge, K., & Baxter, L. A. (1992). Blended friendships: Friends as work associates. *Western Journal of Communication, 56,* 200–225.

Brown, C. (1992, February). A last good place to live: Inside a residence for the homeless with AIDS. *Harper's Magazine,* 48–55.

Brown, M. H. (1985). That reminds me of a story: Speech action in organizational socialization. *Western Journal of Speech Communication, 49,* 27–43.

Buber, M. (1958). *Paths in utopia.* Boston: Beacon Hill.

Budz, T. (1993). Case management. In S. J. Miller, K. I. Ward, & R. Rybicki (Eds.), *Handbook for assisted living* (pp. 75–80). Chicago: Bonaventure House.

Carbaugh, D. (1988a). Cultural terms and tensions in the speech at a television station. *Western Journal of Speech Communication, 52,* 216–237.

Carbaugh, D. (1988b). *Talking American: Cultural discourse on Donahue.* Norwood, NJ: Ablex.

Carrier, J. M., & Magaña, J. R. (1992). Use of ethnosexual data on men of Mexican origin for HIV/AIDS prevention program. In G. Herdt & S. Lindenbaum (Eds.), *The time of AIDS: Social analysis, theory, and method* (pp. 243–258). Newbury Park, CA: Sage.

Cawyer, C. S., & Smith-Dupré, A. (1995). Communicating social support: Identifying supportive episodes in an HIV/AIDS support group. *Communication Quarterly, 43,* 243–258.

Chao, G. T., O'Leary-Kelly, A. M., Wolf, S., Klein, H. J., & Gardner, P. D. (1994). Organizational socialization: Its content and consequences. *Journal of Applied Psychology, 79,* 730–743.

Charmaz, K. (1987). Struggling for a self: Identity levels of the chronically ill. *Research in the Sociology of Health Care, 6,* 283–321.

Charmaz, K. (1991). *Good days, bad days: The self in chronic illness and time.* New Brunswick, NJ: Rutgers University Press.

Cheney, G. (1983). The rhetoric of identification and the study of organizational communication. *Quarterly Journal of Speech, 69,* 143–158.

Cheney, G. (1991). *Rhetoric in an organizational society: Managing multiple identities.* Columbia: University of South Carolina Press.

Cheney, G. (1992). The corporate person represents itself. In E. L. Toth & R. L. Heath (Eds.), *Rhetorical and critical approaches to public relations* (pp. 165–183). Hillsdale, NJ: Lawrence Erlbaum Associates.

Cheney, G., & Tompkins, P. (1987). Coming to terms with organizational identification and commitment. *Central States Speech Journal, 38,* 1–15.

Cheney, G., & Vibbert, S. L. (1987). Corporate discourse: Public relations and issue management. In F. M. Jablin, L. L. Putnam, K. H. Roberts, & L. W. Porter (Eds.), *Handbook of organizational communication* (pp. 165–194). Newbury Park, CA: Sage.

Chesler, M. A., & Barbarin, O. A. (1984). Difficulties of providing help in a crisis: Relationships between parents of children with cancer and their friends. *Journal of Social Issues, 40,* 113–134.

Christensen, L. T., & Cheney, G. (1994). Articulating identity in an organizational age. In S. A. Deetz (Ed.), *Communication yearbook 17* (pp. 222–235). Thousand Oaks, CA: Sage.

Cissna, K., Cox, D. E., & Bochner, A. P. (1990). The dialectic of marital and parental relationships within the stepfamily. *Communication Monographs, 57,* 46–61.

Cleveland, P. H. (1987, November). *AIDS: A strain on family relationships.* Paper presented at the meeting of the National Council on Family Relations, Atlanta, GA.

Cline, R. J., & Boyd, M. F. (1993). Communication as threat and therapy: Social support, and coping with HIV infection. In E. B. Ray (Ed.), *Case studies in health communication* (pp. 131–147). Hillsdale, NJ: Lawrence Erlbaum Associates.

Cohen, A. P. (1985). *The symbolic construction of community.* London: Routledge.

Coleman, T. (1990). Managing diversity at work: The new American dilemma. *Public Management, 72,* 2–6.

Collopy, B., Boyle, P., & Jennings, B. (1991). New directions in nursing home ethics. *Hastings Center Report, 21* (Special suppl.), 1–16.

Comer, D. (1991). Organizational newcomers' acquisition of information from peers. *Management Communication Quarterly, 5,* 64–89.

Conner, S. R. (1994). Denial, acceptance, and other myths. In I. B. Corless, B. B. Germino, & M. Pittman (Eds.), *Dying, death, and bereavement: Theoretical perspectives and other ways of knowing* (pp. 157–170). Boston: Jones & Bartlett.

Conquergood, D. (1992). Life in Big Red: Struggles and accommodations in a Chicago polyethnic tenement. In L. Lamphere (Ed.), *Structuring diversity: Ethnographic perspectives on the new immigration* (pp. 95–144). Chicago: University of Chicago Press.

Conquergood, D. (1994). Homeboys and hoods: Gang communication and cultural space. In L. R. Frey (Ed.), *Group communication in context: Studies of natural groups* (pp. 23–55). Hillsdale, NJ: Lawrence Erlbaum Associates.

Conrad, C. (1983). Organizational power: Faces and symbolic forms. In L. Putnam & M. Pacanowsky (Eds.), *Communication and organizations: An interpretive approach* (pp. 173–194). Beverly Hills, CA: Sage.

Cox, T., & Blake, S. (1991). Managing cultural diversity: Implications for organizational competitiveness. *Academy of Management Executive, 5,* 45–56.

Crandall, C. S., & Coleman, R. (1992). AIDS-related stigmatization and the disruption of social relationships. *Journal of Social and Personal Relationships, 9,* 163–177.

Crimp, D. (1992). Portraits of people with AIDS. In L. Grossberg, C. Nelson, & P. Treichler (Eds.), *Cultural studies* (pp. 117–133). New York: Routledge.

Csikszentmihalyi, M., & Rochberg-Halton, E. (1981). *The meaning of things: Domestic symbols and the self.* Cambridge, England: Cambridge University Press.

Czarniawska-Jorges, B. (1994). Narratives of individual and organizational identities. In S. A. Deetz (Ed.), *Communication yearbook 17* (pp. 193–221). Thousand Oaks, CA: Sage.

Dandridge, T. C., Mitroff, I., & Joyce, W. F. (1980). Organizational symbolism: A topic to expand organizational analysis. *Academy of Management Review, 5,* 77–82.

Davidson, L. (1990). *The Alexian Brothers of Chicago: An evolutionary look at the monastery and modern health care.* New York: Vantage Press.

Deetz, S. A. (1992). *Democracy in an age of corporate colonization.* Albany: State University of New York Press.

Dervin, B. (1983, May). *An overview of sense-making research: Concepts, methods and results to date.* Paper presented at the meeting of the International Communication Association, Dallas, TX.

de Tocqueville, A. (1969). *Democracy in America* (2 Vols., G. Lawrence, Trans.). New York: Doubleday. (Original work published 1841)

DiDomenico, M. J. (1993). Pastoral care at Bonaventure House. In S. J. Miller, K. I. Ward, & R. Rybicki (Eds.), *Handbook for assisted living* (pp. 111–120). Chicago: Bonaventure House.

Donnellon, A., Gray, B., & Bongon, M. G. (1986). Communication, meaning, and organized action. *Administrative Science Quarterly, 31,* 43–55.

Dreuilh, E. (1988). *Mortal embrace: Living with AIDS.* New York: Hill & Wang.

Durkheim, E. (1965). *The elementary forms of the religious life.* New York: The Free Press.

Eisenberg, E. M. (1994). Dialogue as democratic discourse: Affirming Harrison. In S. A. Deetz (Ed.), *Communication yearbook 17* (pp. 275–284). Thousand Oaks, CA: Sage.

Eisenberg, E. M., & Goodall, H. L., Jr. (1994). *Organizational communication: Balancing creativity and constraint.* New York: St. Martin's Press.

Engel, G. (1968). A life setting conducive to illness: The giving-in given-up complex. *Annals of Internal Medicine, 69,* 293–300.

Engel, G. (1971). Sudden and rapid death from psychological stress. *Annals of Internal Medicine, 74,* 771–782.

Erikson, E. (1976). *Everything in its path.* New York: Simon & Shuster.

Etzioni, A. (1993). *The spirit of community: The reinvention of American society.* New York: Touchstone.

Farmer, P. (1992). New disorder, old dilemmas: AIDS and anthropology in Haiti. In G. Herdt & S. Lindenbaum (Eds.), *The time of AIDS: Social analysis, theory, and method* (pp. 287–318). Newbury Park, CA: Sage.

Fernandez, J. P. (1991). *Managing a diverse work force*. Lexington, MA: Lexington.

Fineberg, H. V. (1988, October). The social dimensions of AIDS. *Scientific American*, 128–134.

Finnegan, C. A. (1995, November). *Threads of charity: The NAMES Project AIDS Memorial Quilt in a comic frame*. Paper presented at the meeting of the Speech Communication Association, San Antonio, TX.

Fisher, J. D., Goff, B. A., Nadler, A., & Chinsky, J. M. (1988). Social psychological influences on help seeking and support from peers. In B. H. Gottlieb (Ed.), *Marshaling social support: Formats, processes, and effects* (pp. 267–304). Newbury Park, CA: Sage.

Fisher, W. R. (1984). Narration as a human communication paradigm: The case of public moral argument. *Communication Monographs*, *51*, 1–22.

Fisher, W. R. (1987). *Human communication as narration: Toward a philosophy of reason, value, and action*. Columbia: University of South Carolina Press.

Foucault, M. (1979). *Discipline and punish* (A. Sheridan, Trans.). New York: Vintage.

Fowler, R. B. (1991). *The dance with community: The contemporary debate in American political thought*. Lawrence: University of Kansas Press.

Fowler, R. B. (1995). Community: Reflections on definition. In A. Etzioni (Ed.), *New communitarian thinking: Persons, virtues, institutions, and communities* (pp. 88–95). Charlottesville: University Press of Virginia.

Frake, C. O. (1977). Plying frames can be dangerous: Reflections on methodology in cognitive anthropology. *Quarterly Newsletter of the Institute for Comparative Human Development*, *3*, 1–7.

Freund, P. E. S., & McGuire, M. B. (1995). *Health, illness, and the social body: A critical sociology* (2nd ed.). Englewood Cliffs, NJ: Prentice-Hall.

Frey, L. R. (1994). The naturalistic paradigm: Studying small groups in the postmodern era. *Small Group Research*, *25*, 551–577.

Frey, L. R., & Adelman, M. B. (1993). Building community life: Understanding individual, group, and organizational processes. In S. J. Miller, K. I. Ward, & R. Rybicki (Eds.), *Handbook for assisted living* (pp. 31–40). Chicago: Bonaventure House.

Frey, L. R., Adelman, M. B., & Query, J. L., Jr. (1996). Communication practices in the social construction of health in an AIDS residence. *Journal of Health Psychology*, *1*, 383–397.

Frey, L. R., & Barge, J. K. (Eds.). (1997). *Managing group life: Communicating in decision-making groups*. Boston: Houghton Mifflin.

Friedman, M. (1986). Foreword. In R. C. Arnett, *Communication and community: Implications of Martin Buber's dialogue* (pp. vii–xix). Carbondale: Southern Illinois University Press.

Fuoss, K. W. (1995). "Community" contested, imagined, and performed: Cultural performance, contestation, and community in an organized-labor social drama. *Text and Performance Quartely*, *15*, 79–98.

Gagnon, J. H. (1989). Disease and desire. *Daedalus*, *118*, 47–77.

Gagnon, J. H. (1992). Epidemics and researchers: AIDS and the practice of social studies. In G. Herdt & S. Lindenbaum (Eds.), *The time of AIDS: Social analysis, theory, and method* (pp. 27–40). Newbury Park, CA: Sage.

Gallie, W. B. (1964). *Philosophy and historical understanding*. New York: Schocken.

Gardner, C. B. (1991). Stigma and the public self: Notes on communication, self, and others. *Journal of Contemporary Ethnography*, *20*, 251–262.

Geertz, C. (1973). *The interpretation of cultures*. New York: Basic Books.

Geist, P., & Dreyer, J. (1993). The demise of dialogue: A critique of medical encounter ideology. *Western Journal of Communication*, *57*, 233–246.

Gergen, K. J. (1991). *The saturated self: Dilemmas of identity in contemporary life*. New York: Basic Books.

Goffman, E. (1959). *The presentation of self in everyday life*. Garden City, NY: Doubleday.

Goffman, E. (1963). *Stigma: Notes on the management of spoiled identity*. Englewood Cliffs, NJ: Prentice-Hall.

Goldsmith, D. (1990). A dialectical perspective on the expression of autonomy and connection in romantic relationships. *Western Journal of Speech Communication*, *54*, 537–556.

Goldsmith, D. (1994). The role of facework in supportive communication. In B. R. Burleson, T. L. Albrecht, & I. G. Sarason (Eds.), *Communication of social support: Messages, interactions, relationships, and community* (pp. 29–49). Thousand Oaks, CA: Sage.

Gordon, J. B., & Pavlis, S. D. (1989). In need of comfort: AIDS patients in psychiatric units. In I. B. Corless & M. Pittman-Linderman (Eds.), *AIDS: Principles, practices and politics* (pp. 261–278). New York: Hemisphere.

Gottlieb, B. H. (1988). Marshaling social support: The state of the art in research and practice. In B. H. Gottlieb (Ed.), *Marshaling social support: Formats, processes, and effects* (pp. 11–52). Newbury Park, CA: Sage.

Greenberg, M. S., & Shapiro, S. P. (1971). Indebtedness: An adverse aspect of asking for and receiving help. *Sociometry, 34*, 290–301.

Griffin, J. L. (1995, August 30). Survivors' guilt. *Chicago Tribune*, Section 5, pp. 1, 5.

Guba, E. G. (1992). The alternative paradigm dialog. In E. G. Guba (Ed.), *The paradigm dialog* (pp. 17–27). Newbury Park, CA: Sage.

Habenstein, R. W., & Lamars, W. M. (1963). *Funeral customs the world over*. Milwaukee, WI: Bulfin.

Hawkins, A. H. (1993). *Reconstructing illness: Studies in pathography*. West Lafayette, IN: Purdue University Press.

Hawley, A. H. (1984). Sociological human ecology: Past, present and future. In M. Micklin & H. M. Choldin (Eds.), *Sociological human ecology: Contemporary issues and applications* (pp. 1–19). Boulder, CO: Westview Press.

Herdt, G. (1992). Introduction. In G. Herdt & S. Lindenbaum (Eds.), *The time of AIDS: Social analysis, theory, and method* (pp. 3–26). Newbury Park, CA: Sage.

Holmes, T. H., & Rahe, R. H. (1967). The social readjustment rating scale. *Journal of Psychosomatic Research, 11*, 213–218.

Hughes, E. C. (1958). *Men and their work*. New York: The Free Press.

Hunter, A. (1974). *Symbolic communities: The persistence and change of Chicago's local communities*. Chicago: University of Chicago Press.

Hyman, R. B., Bulkin, W., & Woog, P. C. (1993). The staff's perception of a skilled nursing facility. *Qualitative Health Research, 3*, 209–235.

Jablin, F. (1987). Organizational entry, assimilation and exit. In F. M. Jablin, L. L. Putnam, K. Roberts, & L. Porter (Eds.), *Handbook of organizational communication* (pp. 679–740). Newbury Park, CA: Sage.

Jackson, S. E., & Associates (1992). *Diversity in the workplace: Human resource initiatives*. New York: Guilford.

Jeffres, L. W., Dobos, J., & Sweeney, M. (1987). Communication and commitment to community. *Communication Research, 14*, 619–643.

Jemmott, J. B., III, & Locke, S. E. (1984). Psychosocial factors, immunologic mediation, and human susceptibility to infectious diseases: How much do we know? *Psychological Bulletin, 95*, 78–108.

Kaminer, W., (1992). *I'm dysfunctional, you're dysfunctional: The recovery movement and other self-help fashions*. Reading, MA: Addison-Wesley.

Kanter, R. M. (1968). Commitment and social organization: A study of commitment mechanisms in utopian communities. *American Sociological Review, 33*, 499–517.

Kanter, R. M. (1972). *Commitment and community: Communes and utopias in sociological perspective*. Cambridge, MA: Harvard University Press.

Kaplan, B. H., Cassel, J. C., & Gore, S. (1977). Social support and health. *Medical Care, 15*, 47–58.

Kaplan, R. M., & Toshima, M. T. (1990). The functional effects of social relationships on chronic illnesses and disability. In B. R. Sarason, I. G. Sarason, & G. R. Pierce (Eds.), *Social support: An interactional view* (pp. 427–454). New York: Wiley.

Karp, D. A. (1994). The dialectics of depression. *Symbolic Interaction, 17*, 341–366.

Kastenbaum, R. (1969). Death and bereavement in later life. In A. H. Kutscher (Ed.), *Death and bereavement* (pp. 28–54). Springfield, IL: Thomas.

Kastenbaum, R. (1994). Is there an ideal deathbed scene? In I. B. Corless, B. B. Germino, & M. Pittman (Eds.), *Dying, death and bereavement: Theoretical perspectives and other ways of knowing* (pp. 109–122). Boston: Jones & Bartlett.

Katriel, T. (1991). *Communal webs: Communication and culture in contemporary Israel*. Albany: State University of New York Press.

Katriel, T., & Farrell, T. (1991). Scrapbooks as cultural texts: An American art of memory. *Text and Performance Quarterly, 11*, 1–17.

Katriel, T., & Philipsen, G. (1981). "What we need is communication": "Communication" as a cultural category in some American speech. *Communication Monographs, 48,* 301–317.

Kelly, J., & Sykes, P. (1989). Helping the helpers: A support group for family members of persons with AIDS. *Social Work, 34,* 239–242.

Kirchmeyer, C. (1993). Multicultural task groups: An account of the low contribution levels of minorities. *Small Group Research, 24,* 127–148.

Kirchmeyer, C., & Cohen, A. (1992). Multicultural groups: Their performance and reactions with constructive conflict. *Group & Organization Management, 17,* 153–170.

Kleck, R. E. (1968). Self-disclosure patterns of the nonobviously stigmatized. *Psychological Reports, 23,* 1239–1248.

Klonoff, E., & Ewers, D. (1990). Care of AIDS patients as a source of stress to nursing staff. *AIDS Education and Prevention, 2,* 338–348.

Koch, S., & Deetz, S. (1981). Metaphor analysis of social reality in organizations. *Journal of Applied Communication Research, 9,* 1–15.

La Gapia, J. J. (1990). The negative effects of informal support systems. In S. Duck (Ed., with R. Silver), *Personal relationships and social support* (pp. 122–139). London: Sage.

Lakoff, G., & Johnson, M. (1980). *Metaphors we live by.* Chicago: University of Chicago Press.

Larwood, L. (1992). Don't struggle to scope those metaphors yet. *Group & Organization Management, 17,* 249–254.

Lehman, D. R., Ellard, J. H., & Wortman, C. B. (1986). Social support for the bereaved: Recipient's and provider's perspectives on what is helpful. *Journal of Consulting and Clinical Psychology, 54,* 483–446.

Lewan, L. S. (1990). Diversity in the workplace. *HRMagazine, 35,* 42–49.

Lincoln, Y. S., & Guba, E. G. (1985). *Naturalistic inquiry.* Beverly Hills, CA: Sage.

Littlejohn, S. W. (1996). *Theories of human communication* (5th ed.). Belmont, CA: Wadsworth.

Littlewood, J. (1992). *Aspects of grief: Bereavement in adult life.* London: Tavistock/Routledge.

Louis, M. (1980). Surprise and sense making: What newcomers experience in entering unfamiliar organizational settings. *Administrative Science Quarterly, 25,* 226–251.

Lupton, D. (1993). AIDS risk and heterosexuality in the Australian press. *Discourse & Society, 4,* 307–328.

Lupton, D. (1994). Toward the development of critical health communication praxis. *Health Communication, 6,* 55–67.

MacIntyre, A. (1981). *After virtue: A study in moral theory* (2nd ed.). Notre Dame, IN: University of Notre Dame Press.

Maione, M., & McKee, J. (1987). AIDS: Implications for counselors. *Journal of Humanistic Education and Development, 26,* 12–23.

Marcus, G. E., & Fischer, M. M. J. (1986). *Anthropology as cultural critique: An experimental moment in the human sciences.* Chicago: University of Chicago Press.

Martin, J. (1982). Stories and scripts in organizational settings. In A. Hastorf & I. Isen (Eds.), *Cognitive social psychology* (pp. 205–225). New York: Elsevier-North Holland.

Martin, J. L., & Dean, L. (1993). Bereavement following death from AIDS: Unique problems, reactions, and special needs. In M. S. Stroebe, W. Stroebe, & R. O. Hansson (Eds.), *Handbook of bereavement: Theory, research and intervention* (pp. 317–330). New York: Cambridge University Press.

Masheter, C. (1994). Dialogues between ex-spouses: The roles of attachment and interpersonal conflict. In R. Conville (Ed.), *Uses of "structure" in communication studies* (pp. 83–101). New York: Praeger.

Masheter, C., & Harris, L. (1986). From divorce to friendship: A study of dialectical relationship development. *Journal of Social and Personal Relationships, 3,* 177–179.

McAlexander, J. J. (1991). Divorce, the disposition of the relationships, and everything. In R. Holman & M. R. Solomon (Eds.), *Advances in consumer research* (Vol. 18, pp. 43–48). Provo, UT: Association for Consumer Research.

McAlexander, J. J., Schouten, J. W., & Roberts, S. D. (1993). Consumer behavior and divorce. In J. A. Costa & R. W. Belk (Eds.), *Research in consumer behavior* (Vol. 6, pp. 185–230). Greenwich, CT: JAI.

McKinlay, J. B. (1973). Social networks, lay consultation and help-seeking behavior. *Social Forces, 51,* 275–292.

McLeroy, K. R., DeVellis, R., DeVellis, B., Kaplan, B., & Toole, J. (1984). Social support and physical recovery in a stroke population. *Journal of Social and Personal Relationships, 1*, 395–413.

McMillan, D. W., & Chavis, D. M. (1986). Sense of community: A definition and theory. *Journal of Community Psychology, 14*, 6–23.

Merideth, P. (1992a, March 27). "Faces of AIDS" documents an oasis of support. *Chicago Tribune*, Section 7, p. 79.

Merideth, P. (1992b, March 27). Faces of AIDS: Life and death at Bonaventure House. *Chicago Reader*, Section 1, pp. 1, 9–11.

Merideth, P. (1992c, March 23–May 23). Faces of AIDS: The Bonaventure House project [Exhibit]. Chicago Cultural Center.

Merton, T. (1961). *New seeds of contemplation*. New York: New Directions.

Meyer, J. (1995). Tell me a story: Eliciting organizational values from narratives. *Communication Quarterly, 43*, 210–224.

Meyrowitz, J. (1985). *No sense of place: The impact of electronic media on social behavior*. Oxford, England: Oxford University Press.

Miller, R. J. (1991). Some notes on the impact of treating AIDS patients in hospices. In M. O'Rawe Amenta (Ed.), *AIDS and the hospice community* (pp. 1–12). Binghamton, NY: Harrington Park Press.

Miller, S. J., Ward, K. I., & Rybicki, R. (1993). Introduction. In S. J. Miller, K. I. Ward, & R. Rybicki (Eds.), *Handbook for assisted living* (pp. 13–15). Chicago: Bonaventure House.

Miller, V., & Jablin, F. (1991). Information-seeking during organizational entry: Influences, tactics, and a model of the process. *Academy of Management Review, 16*, 92–120.

Moore, S. F. (1975). Epilogue: Uncertainties in situations, indeterminacies in culture. In S. F. Moore & B. G. Myerhoff (Eds.), *Symbol and politics in communal ideology: Cases and questions* (pp. 210–239). Ithaca, NY: Cornell University Press.

Morgan, G. (1986). *Images of organizations*. Beverly Hills, CA: Sage.

Morrison, E. W. (1993). Newcomer information-seeking: Exploring types, modes, sources, and outcomes. *Academy of Management Journal, 36*, 557–589

Morrison, E. W. (1995). Information usefulness and acquisition during organizational encounter. *Management Communication Quarterly, 9*, 131–155.

Mowday, J. H., Steers, R. M., & Porter, L. W. (1979). The measurement of organizational commitment. *Journal of Vocational Behavior, 14*, 227–247.

Mumby, D. K. (1993). Critical organizational communication studies: The next 10 years. *Communication Monographs, 60*, 18–25.

Mumby, D. K., & Stohl, C. (1991). Power and discourse in organizational studies: Absence and the dialectic of control. *Discourse and Society, 2*, 313–332.

Murphy, R. F. (1971). *The dialectics of social life*. New York: Basic Books.

Myerhoff, B. G. (1975). Organization and ecstasy: Deliberate and accidental communitas among Hichol Indians and American youth. In S. F. Moore & B. G. Myeroff (Eds.), *Symbol and politics in communal ideology: Cases and questions* (pp. 33–67). Ithaca, NY: Cornell University Press.

Myerhoff, B. G. (1978). *Number our days*. New York: Simon & Schuster.

Myerhoff, B. G. (1982). Life history among the elderly: Performance, visibility, and re-membering. In J. Ruby (Ed.), *A crack in the mirror: Reflexive perspectives in anthropology* (pp. 99–117). Philadelphia: University of Pennsylvania Press.

Norton, R. (1975). Measurement of ambiguity tolerance. *Journal of Personality Assessment, 39*, 607–619.

Norton, R., Schwartzbaum, J., & Wheat, J. (1990). Language discrimination of general physicians: AIDS metaphors used in the AIDS crisis. *Communication Research, 17*, 809–826.

Nussbaum, M. C. (1994). *The therapy of desire: Theory and practice in Hellenistic ethics*. Princeton, NJ: Princeton University Press.

Ochs, D. J. (1993). *Consolatory rhetoric: Grief, symbol and ritual in the Greco-Roman era*. Columbia: University of South Carolina Press.

Ojanlatva, A., Cochrane, L., & Walker, A. (1991). *Training volunteers for an AIDS buddy program*. Turka, Finland: Department of Public Health, University of Turka. (ERIC Document Reproduction Service No. ED 335 378)

Olson, C. D. (1985). Materialism in the home: The impact of artifacts on dyadic communication. In E. C. Hirschman & M. B. Holbrook (Eds.) *Advances in consumer research*, (Vol. 12, pp. 388–393). Provo, UT: Association for Consumer Research.

Ostroff, C., & Kozlowski, W. J. (1992). Organizational socialization as a learning process: The role of information acquisition. *Personnel Psychology, 45*, 42–65.

O'Sullivan, T., Hartley, J., Saunders, D., Montgomery, M., & Fiske, J. (1994). *Key concepts in communication and cultural studies* (2nd ed.). London: Routledge.

Parkes, C. M. (1993). Bereavement as a psychosocial transition: Processes of adaptation to change. In M. S. Stroebe, W. Stroebe, & R. O. Hansson (Eds.), *Handbook of bereavement: Theory, research and intervention* (pp. 91–101). New York: Cambridge University Press.

Parks, M. R. (1995). Ideology in interpersonal communication: Beyond the couches, talk shows, and bunkers. In B. R. Burleson (Ed.), *Communication yearbook 18* (pp. 480–497). Thousand Oaks, CA: Sage.

Patton, C. (1990). *Inventing AIDS*. London: Routledge.

Pearce, W. B. (1989). *Communication and the human condition*. Carbondale: Southern Illinois University Press.

Pfeiffer, J. (1981). Management as symbolic action: The creation and maintenance of organizational paradigms. In L. L. Cummings & B. Staw (Eds.), *Research in organizational behavior* (Vol. 3, pp. 1–52). Greenwich, CT: JAI.

Philipsen, G. (1987). The prospect for cultural communication. In D. L. Kincaid (Ed.), *Communication theory: Eastern and Western perspectives* (pp. 245–254). New York: Academic Press.

Pilisuk, M., & Parks, S. H. (1986). *The healing web: Social networks and human survival*. Hanover, NH: University Press of New England.

Poole, M. S., Seibold, D. R., & McPhee, R. D. (1986). A structurational approach to theory-building in group decision-making research. In R. Y. Hirokawa & M. S. Poole (Eds.), *Communication and group decision-making* (pp. 237–264). Beverly Hills, CA: Sage.

Proctor, D. E. (1990). The dynamic spectacle: Transforming experience into social forms of community. *Quarterly Journal of Speech, 76*, 117–133.

Query, J. L., Jr. (1987). *A field test of the relationship between interpersonal communication competence, number of social supports, and satisfaction with the social support received by an elderly support group*. Unpublished master's thesis, Ohio University, Athens.

Quimby, E. (1992). Anthropological witnessing for African Americans: Power, responsibility, and choice in the age of AIDS. In G. Herdt & S. Lindenbaum (Eds.), *The time of AIDS: Social analysis, theory, and method* (pp. 159–184). Newbury Park, CA: Sage.

Quindlen, A. (1993, October 17). America's sleeping sickness. *New York Times*, Section 4, p. 17.

Rawlins, W. K. (1983). Negotiating close friendship: The dialectic of conjunctive freedoms. *Human Communication Research, 9*, 255–266.

Rawlins, W. K. (1989). A dialectical analysis of the tensions, functions, and strategic challenges of communication in young adult friendships. In J. A. Anderson (Ed.), *Communication yearbook 12* (pp. 157–189). Newbury Park, CA: Sage.

Rawlins, W. K. (1992). *Friendship matters: Communication, dialectics, and the life course*. New York: Aldine.

Redman, P. (1991). Invasion of the monstrous others: Identity, genre and HIV. *Cultural Studies from Birmingham, 1*, 8–28.

Rheingold, H. (1993). *The virtual community: Homesteading on the electronic frontier*. New York: HarperPerennial.

Riley, P. (1983). A structurationist account of political culture. *Administrative Science Quarterly, 28*, 414–437.

Riley, P. (1985). Spinning on symbolism: The spinning metaphor and dialectical tension. *Journal of Management, 11*, 49–50.

Roberts, J. (1988). Setting the frame: Definition, functions, and typology of rituals. In E. Imber-Black, J. Roberts, & R. A. Whiting (Eds.), *Rituals in families and family therapy* (pp. 3–46). New York: Norton.

Rook, K. S. (1984). The negative side of social interaction: Impact on psychological well-being. *Journal of Personality and Social Psychology, 46*, 1097–1108.

Rosenblatt, P. C. (1993). Grief: The social context of private feelings. In M. S. Stroebe, W. Stroebe, & R. O. Hansson (Eds.), *Handbook of bereavement: Theory, research, and intervention* (pp. 102–111). New York: Cambridge University Press.

Ross, J. W. (1989). An ethics of compassion, a language of division: Working out the AIDS metaphors. In I. B. Corless & M. Pittman-Lindeman (Eds.), *AIDS: Principles, practices and politics* (pp. 351–363). New York: Hemisphere.

Rothenbuhler, E. W. (1991). The process of community involvement. *Communication Monographs, 58,* 63–78.

Ruhe, J., & Eatman, J. (1977). Effects of racial composition on small work groups. *Small Group Behavior, 8,* 479–486.

Ruskin, C. (1988). *The quilt: Stories from the NAMES Project.* New York: Pocket Books.

Rychlak, J. F. (Ed.). (1976). *Dialectic: Humanistic rationale for behavior and development.* Basel, Switzerland: D. Karter.

Sackmann, S. A. (1989). The role of metaphors in organization transformation. *Human Relations, 42,* 463–485.

Sackmann, S. A. (1990). Managing organizational culture: Dreams and possibilities. In J. A. Anderson (Ed.), *Communication yearbook 13* (pp. 114–148). Newbury Park, CA: Sage.

Sass, J. S., & Canary, D. J. (1991). Organizational commitment and identification: An examination of conceptual and operational convergence. *Western Journal of Speech Communication, 55,* 275–293.

Scheerhorn, D. (1990). Hemophilia in the days of AIDS: Communicative tensions surrounding associated stigmas. *Communication Research, 17,* 842–847.

Schietinger, H. (1988). Housing for people with AIDS. *Death Studies, 12,* 481–499.

Schneider, J. W., & Conrad, P. (1983). *Having epilepsy: The experience and control of illness.* Philadelphia: Temple University Press.

Schutz, W. C. (1960). *FIRO: A three-dimensional theory of interpersonal behavior.* New York: Holt, Rinehart, & Winston.

Sennett, R. (1980). *Authority.* New York: Random House.

Shaffer, C. R., & Anundsen, K. (1993). *Creating community anywhere: Finding support and connection in a fragmented world.* New York: Putnam.

Siehl, C. (1985). After the founder: An opportunity to manage culture. In P. J. Frost, L. F. Moore, M. R. Louis, C. C. Lundberg, & J. Martin (Eds.), *Organizational culture* (pp. 125–140). Beverly Hills, CA: Sage.

Sigman, S. J. (1985–86). The applicability of the concept of recruitment to the communications study of a nursing home: An ethnographic case study. *International Journal of Aging and Human Development, 22,* 215–233.

Smith, K. K., & Berg, D. N. (1987). *Paradoxes of group life: Understanding conflict, paralysis, and movement in group dynamics.* San Francisco: Jossey-Bass.

Solomon, G. F. (1987). Psychoneuroimmunologic approaches to research on AIDS. *Annals of the New York Academy of Science, 496,* 628–636.

Solomon, R. C. (1989). The emotions of justice. *Social Justice Research, 3,* 345–374.

Sontag, S. (1989). *Illness as metaphor and AIDS and its metaphors.* New York: Anchor.

Sosnowitz, B., & Appleby, G. (1988, August). *Preventing volunteer burn out through a structured support network.* Paper presented at the meeting of the Society for the Study of Social Problems, Atlanta, GA.

Stohl, C. (1986). The role of memorable messages in the process of organizational socialization. *Communication Quarterly, 34,* 231–249.

Strauss, A. (1982). Interorganizational negotiation. *Urban Life, 11,* 350–367.

Strine, M. S., Long, B. W., & Hopkins, M. F. (1990). Research in interpretation and performance studies: Trends, issues, priorities. In G. M. Phillips & J. T. Wood (Eds.), *Speech communication: Essays to commemorate the 75th anniversary of the Speech Communication Association* (pp. 181–204). Carbondale: Southern Illinois University Press.

Stroebe, W., & Stroebe, M. S. (1987). *Bereavement and health: The psychological and physical consequences of partner loss.* Cambridge, England: Cambridge University Press.

Suczek, B., & Fagenhaugh, S. (1991). AIDS and outreach work. In D. Maines (Ed.), *Social organization and social process: Essays in honor of Anselm Strauss* (pp. 159–173). New York: Aldine Press.

Taylor, S. (1989). *Positive illusions: Creative self deceptions and the healthy mind*. New York: Basic Books.

Taylor, S. E., Falke, R. L., Mazel, R. M., & Hilsberg, B. L. (1988). Sources of satisfaction and dissatisfaction among members of cancer support groups. In B. H. Gottlieb (Ed.), *Marshaling social support: Formats, processes, and effects* (pp. 187–208). Newbury Park, CA: Sage.

Teboul, JC. B. (1994). Facing and coping with uncertainty during organizational entry. *Management Communication Quarterly, 8*, 190–224.

The NAMES Project Foundation (1995, December 3). The NAMES Project: Our history. *AIDS Memorial Quilt Website* (http://www.AIDSquilt.org/history.html).

The NAMES Project Foundation (1996a, July 3). The history of the NAMES Project. *AIDS Memorial Quilt Website* (http://www.AIDSquilt.org/history.html).

The NAMES Project Foundation. (1996b, July 3). The NAMES Project: A message from the NAMES Project founder Clive Jones: A World AIDS day demand for more research. *AIDS Memorial Quilt Website* (http://www.AIDSquilt.org/names/jones.html).

Tilleraas, P. (1988). *The color of light: Meditations for all of us living with AIDS*. San Francisco: Harper & Row.

Tillich, P. (1952). *The courage to be*. New Haven, CT: Yale University Press.

Tinder, G. (1995). *Tolerance and community*. Columbia: University of Missouri Press.

Tompkins, P. K., & Cheney, G. (1985). Communication and unobtrusive control in contemporary organizations. In R. D. McPhee & P. K. Tompkins (Eds.), *Organizational communication: Traditional themes and new directions* (pp. 179–210). Beverly Hills, CA: Sage.

Treadwell, D. F., & Harrison, T. M. (1994). Conceptualizing and assessing organizational image: Model images, commitment, and communication. *Communication Monographs, 61*, 63–85.

Trechsel, G. A. (1990). Mourning quilts in America. In L. Horton (Ed.), *Uncoverings 1989* (pp. 139–158). San Francisco: American Quilt Study Group.

Treichler, P. A. (1987). AIDS, homophobia, and biomedical discourse: An epidemic of signification. *Cultural Studies, 1*, 263–305.

Trujillo, N. (1985). Organizational communication as cultural performance: Some managerial considerations. *Southern Speech Communication Journal, 50*, 201–224.

Turner, V. (1969). *The ritual process: Structure and anti-structure*. Ithaca, NY: Cornell University Press.

Vaid–Raizada, V. K. (1985). Management of interethnic conflict in an Indian manufacturing organization. *Psychological Reports, 56*, 731–738.

van Gennep, A. (1960). *The rites of passage* (M. B. Vizedom & G. L. Chaffee, Trans.). Chicago: University of Chicago Press.

Van Loon, R. A. (1993). Hospice care in a residential facility. In S. J. Miller, K. I. Ward, & R. Rybicki (Eds.), *Handbook for assisted living* (pp. 99–110). Chicago: Bonaventure House.

Van Maanen, J. (1978). People processing: Strategies of organizational socialization. *Organizational Dynamics, 7*, 18–36.

Vaughn, M. A. (1995). Organization symbols: An analysis of their types of functions in a reborn organization. *Management Communication Quarterly, 9*, 219–250.

Watney, S. (1994). *Practices of freedom: Selected writings on HIV/AIDS*. Durham, NC: Duke University Press.

Weick, K. E. (1979). *The social psychology of organizing* (2nd ed.). Reading, MA: Addison-Wesley.

Werner, C. M., & Baxter, L. A. (1994). Temporal qualities of relationships: Organismic, transactional, and dialectical views. In M. L. Knapp & G. R. Millers (Eds.), *Handbook of interpersonal communication* (2nd ed., pp. 323–377). Thousand Oaks, CA: Sage.

Wilkens, A. L. (1984). The creation of company cultures: The role of stories and human resource systems. *Human Resource Management, 23*, 41–60.

Wilmot, W. W. (1987). *Dyadic communication* (3rd ed.). New York: Random House.

Wilson, M. (1957). *Rituals of kinship among the Nyakyusa*. London: Oxford University Press.

Worden, J. W. (1982). *Grief counseling and grief therapy: A handbook for the mental health practitioner*. New York: Springer.

Wortman, C. N. (1984). Social support and the cancer patient: Conceptual and methodological issues. *Cancer, 53*, 2339–2360.

Wortman, C. B., & Lehman, D. R. (1985). Reactions to victims of life crises: Support attempts that fail. In I. G. Sarason & B. R. Sarason (Eds.), *Social support: Theory, research and application* (pp. 464–489). Boston: Martinus Nijhoff.

Wuthnow, R. (1994). *Sharing the journey: Support groups and America's new quest for community.* New York: The Free Press.

Young, I. M. (1995). The ideal of community and the politics of difference. In P. A. Weiss & M. Friedman (Eds.), *Feminism & community* (pp. 233–257). Philadelphia: Temple University Press.

Young, M. M. (1991). Disposition of possessions during role transitions. In R. Holman & M. R. Solomon (Eds.), *Advances in consumer research* (Vol. 18, pp. 33–39). Provo, UT: Association for Consumer Research.

Zablocki, B. D. (1971). *The joyful community: An account of the Bruderhof, a communal movement now in its third generation.* Baltimore: Penguin.

Zelewsky, M., & Venning, L. (1993). Managing professional services. In S. J. Miller, K. I. Ward, & R. Rybicki (Eds.), *Handbook for assisted living* (pp. 81–90). Chicago: Bonaventure House.

Zelizer, B. (1995). Reading the past against the grain: The shape of memory studies. *Critical Studies in Mass Communication, 12,* 214–239.

Zick, J., & Temoshok, L. (1987). Perceptions of social support in men with AIDS and ARC: Relationships with distress and hardiness. *Journal of Applied Social Psychology, 17,* 193–215.

Zook, E. G. (1994). Embodied health and constitutive communication: Toward an authentic conceptualization of health communication. In S. A. Deetz (Ed.), *Communication yearbook 17* (pp. 344–377). Thousand Oaks, CA: Sage.

Author Index

Subject Index

Authors' note: In order to assist readers with diverse interests, we designed this index as both a reference and a map to the topics covered in this text. To do so, we limited the number of major headings, and subsumed related terms under appropriate subheadings.

About the Authors

Mara B. Adelman (PhD, University of Washington) is an Assistant Professor in the Department of Communication at Seattle University. Her primary research is on social support in various contexts, including intimate and nonintimate encounters, and community relationships. Soon after Bonaventure House opened in April 1989, Mara served as a volunteer and later became a researcher at the home. In 1991, she coproduced a documentary video of Bonaventure House, entitled *The Pilgrim Must Embark: Living Together With AIDS*. She has coauthored several articles and papers with Dr. Frey on their research at Bonaventure House, in addition to numerous publications on social support.

Lawrence R. Frey (PhD, University of Kansas) is a Professor in the Communication Department at Loyola University Chicago. His research seeks to revitalize the study of group communication by demonstrating the applied value of research to real-life groups and encouraging the use of naturalistic methods. He started conducting research on Bonaventure House with Dr. Adelman in 1991, and 2 years later became a volunteer, which he still is today. Author and editor of many books, chapters, and articles, his edited text, *Group Communication in Context: Studies of Natural Groups* (1994, Lawrence Erlbaum Associates), received both the 1995 Gerald R. Miller Book Award from the Interpersonal and Small Group Interaction Division, and the 1994 Distinguished Book Award from the Applied Communication Division of the Speech Communication Association.